Links: Twentieth Century World History Books
Series Editor: Robert Wolfson

Anipauu e

GW00535676

Examining the Evidence

Robert Wolfson and J. F. Aylett

Edward Arnold

© Robert Wolfson and J. F. Aylett 1988

First published in Great Britain 1988
by Edward Arnold (Publishers) Ltd
41 Bedford Square, London WC1B 3DQ

Edward Arnold (Australia) Pty Ltd
80 Waverley Road, Caulfield East
Victoria 3145, Australia

British Library Cataloguing in Publication Data
Wolfson, Robert
   Examining the evidence.—(Links:
twentieth century world history books).
   1. Historiography
   I. Title   II. Aylett, J.F.   III. Series
   907   D13

ISBN 0 7131 7627 X

Filmset in 11/12 pt Plantin by
TecSet Ltd, Wallington, Surrey
Printed in Great Britain by
Richard Clay Ltd, Chichester

Acknowledgements

The publishers would like to thank the following for permission to reproduce copyright illustrations:
The Mansell Collection Ltd p 4 top; BBC Hulton Picture Library/The Bettmann Archive pp 4 bottom, 17 (Evening Standard), 23 left and right (Evening Standard), 29, 48 top left & top right; John Frost Historical Newspaper Library, pp 7 (Daily Express), 24 right (Daily Express), 30 (Daily Express), 34 left and right, 39 (Daily Express); Photographed from *Hitler* by Norman Stone, Hodder & Stoughton 1980, p 8; John Topham Picture Library p 9 left & right; British Library Newspaper Library pp 12 (The Sun), 36 (The Rhodesia Herald), 41 left (Daily Telegraph), 48 bottom left & bottom right (Sunday Times/Peter F Hopf/European Press Photos Association), 61 (Sunday Times); Associated Press Ltd p 13 top; Ministry of Defence p 13 bottom; Frank Spooner Pictures pp 16 top & 45 right; Rex Features Ltd, p 16 bottom (The Sun); H.M.S.O. Crown Copyright Reserved, p 18; Punch, p 22; U.S. Information Service, p 24 left; Marvin Lyons, p 26; Novosti Press Agency, p 32; Syndication International Ltd pp 35, 41 bottom right; Mail Newspapers plc pp 40 top, 59; Robert Hunt Library/Black Star, pp 40 bottom, 50 top left; The Guardian p 42 top left; The Encyclopedia Britannica, p 42 top left (Papas/the Guardian), p 42 top right (Die Welt), p 42 bottom left (Justus/Minneapolis Star), p 42 bottom right (Sankei Shimbun); The Imperial War Museum pp 43 top left, 45 left; The British Museum, p 43 bottom; Christopher Pullitz/Impact, p 46 top; Robert Hunt Library, p 46 bottom; Heinrich Hoffman, p 47 top; David King Collection, p 47 bottom; National Film Archive, London pp 50 top right, 50 bottom, 51, 52; South Africa Department of Information, 1973, p 60 top left; International Defence & Aid Fund, pp 60 top right, 62; The South African Embassy, p 60 bottom right; David Evans, cover.

Preface

Contents

This book, which is designed for students following GCSE Modern World History courses, will complement existing titles in the *Links* series. By examining the problems associated with the understanding and use of documentary evidence within the context of important twentieth-century topics, it will prepare students for an essential part of the GCSE exam. It covers most forms of twentieth-century sources available and examines in detail their advantages and disadvantages. For reasons of space, fiction, song and radio broadcasts have had to be omitted.

Extensive exercises in each section are specifically designed to meet GCSE assessment objectives, especially objective 4: to use the skills necessary to study a variety of historical evidence by comprehending and extracting information, by interpreting and evaluating (for example, distinguishing between fact, opinion and judgement, detecting bias and identifying gaps in the evidence), and by comparing different types of historical evidence and drawing conclusions from such comparisons.

Inevitably, it has not been possible to include every topic from the extensive *Links* series. Nevertheless, we hope that the book captures something of the fascination of historical study and, in so doing, encourages students to carry out research of their own.

Robert Wolfson and John Aylett

Note: The words which appear in **bold type** in the text are defined in the Glossary on pages 63-4.

1
Sources for Twentieth Century History

You will already have come across the great variety of sources available for historians to study different subjects. The cartoons on pages 5 and 6 will remind you of many of these. Study them now before considering the exercises below.

The Spanish Armada.

Hiroshima, after the atomic bomb.

Exercises

1   If you were asked to find out about the Spanish Armada of 1588 or about the dropping of the atomic bomb on Hiroshima in 1945, and write up your findings, which do you think would be easier to do? Of course plenty of books have been written about each, but if they didn't exist, or you wanted to find out new things, where would you turn to? Using the strip cartoons to give you ideas, write down two lists, one headed 'Sources of information for researching the Spanish Armada', and the other 'Sources of information for researching the atom bomb'.

2   From the first exercise, it is easy to see that there are countless sources available for studying the history of the 20th century, and certainly more than for the earlier period. In many ways, this makes it much easier to find out what happened more recently. But now try answering this question:
In what ways does having *more* sources of information make the historian's task more *difficult*?

PERSONAL EVIDENCE

DIARIES

LETTERS

BIOGRAPHIES

ORAL HISTORY

GOVERNMENT AND OFFICIAL RECORDS

REPORTS OF
PARLIAMENTARY
DEBATES

INTERNATIONAL
TREATIES

GOVERNMENT
REPORTS AND
INVESTIGATIONS

SPEECHES BY
POLITICIANS

STATISTICS

NEWSPAPERS AND MAGAZINES

REPORTS OF
WHAT HAPPENED

EDITORIAL
COMMENTS

FEATURES AND
REVIEWS

LETTERS TO
THE EDITOR

VISUAL EVIDENCE

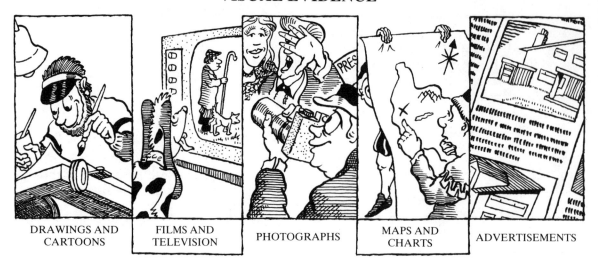

DRAWINGS AND CARTOONS

FILMS AND TELEVISION

PHOTOGRAPHS

MAPS AND CHARTS

ADVERTISEMENTS

ARTEFACTS

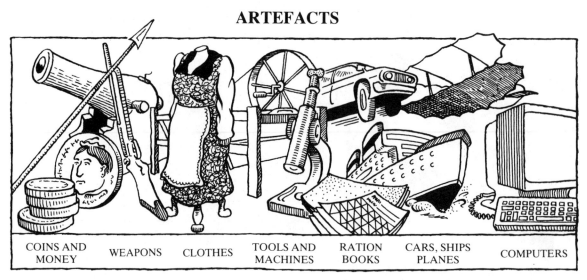

COINS AND MONEY

WEAPONS

CLOTHES

TOOLS AND MACHINES

RATION BOOKS

CARS, SHIPS PLANES

COMPUTERS

OTHER FORMS OF EVIDENCE

LITERARY EVIDENCE

SONGS

RADIO BROADCASTS

HISTORIC SITES — BUILDINGS AND BATTLEFIELDS

What do you want to know?

Of course, we always assume that historians chiefly want to know 'what happened'. We expect them to want to form a **narrative** of events. But it is not quite as simple as that. They have to decide, from all the things that happened, what is important enough to go in the history books. The next exercise illustrates this problem.

Exercise

3 The following six events were all reported in the *Daily Express* on 7 June 1944. Which one do you think was the main news that day? Give reasons for your choice.

(a) Colonel Beck, the former Polish foreign minister, has died of pneumonia.

(b) The Germans have increased the **curfew** in certain areas of France.

(c) Landings on the French beaches were successful and Allied tanks are now 10 miles inland.

(d) Germany has reported that Allied troops have landed in Jersey and Guernsey.

(e) 600 French Communists were rounded up yesterday.

(f) A Bren gun carrier blew up at Colchester, killing one man and injuring another. Two houses were demolished.

Most people will have selected the Allied landings in Normandy, as these were the events that were to lead to the end of the Second World War. But it is also important to consider the question: 'Important to *whom*?' The family of the man killed in Colchester when the Bren carrier blew up may not have been very bothered by the D-Day landings.

As well as having to choose which events to write about, historians ask other questions too:

— *Why* did things happen as they did?
— *What* effects did events have on people?
— *How* did they affect later events?
— *What were they like* for the people who lived through them?

This picture accompanied one of the stories above – which one?

Some took off with new stripes still wet

2
Primary and Secondary Sources

The simple distinction between primary and secondary sources is something you will have learnt before – primary sources come from the time of an event, whereas secondary sources are written or made after the event. However, this does not make them exactly the same as 'first-hand' and 'second-hand' information.

Information about an event could be received from someone else, making it second-hand, but then be set down at the time of the event, making it a primary source. In this chapter, some of the other difficulties of primary and secondary sources are examined. But first complete the exercise below.

Exercise
1 Make two lists, one headed 'Primary sources' and the other 'Secondary sources'. Then place each of the following under the correct heading:
  S (a) A film of the events of the Russian Revolution, made in 1932.
  P (b) A First World War soldier's uniform.
  S (c) *Hitler* by Norman Stone, a book published in 1980.
  P (d) The television news broadcast that included the report and film of Neil Armstrong's walk on the moon in 1969.
  P (e) An Italian Fascist flag, captured in 1943.
  P (f) *Mein Kampf* by Adolf Hitler, published in 1924.
  P (g) A photograph of Neville Chamberlain returning from Germany in 1938.

INTRODUCTION BY J.H.PLUMB
HITLER
BY NORMAN STONE

  P (h) Petrol rationing coupons from the time of the Suez crisis in 1956.
  S (i) *The Bridge at Remagen*, an American film made in the 1970s about the last months of the Second World War.
  P (j) The Treaty of Versailles, 1919.

You probably did not find it difficult to complete this exercise. It is easy enough to identify which items actually come from the time of the event, and which do not.

However, it is not always easy to make this distinction. Look at the photographs above. The photograph of the First World War trench is obviously a primary source. It was actually taken in 1916 and shows us the conditions in which some soldiers lived and fought.

But what about the second picture, which shows the same piece of ground in France today? You could say that it is a primary source because it comes from the time of the event.

On the other hand, look at all the grass which has grown over it. The area around the trench has changed, too. So we certainly don't get much of an idea of what it was like for the soldiers.

Does this make it a secondary source?

Exercise
2 Place each of the following into the primary or secondary category. In each case, explain the *reasons* for your decision.
   (a) A collection of written sources and photographs about Britain in the 1950s. All were written or taken during that **decade**, but collected and published by a historian in 1986.
   (b) A television programme about the Watergate scandal of 1973, made in 1980. It included TV news reports from 1973, interviews with politicians and journalists who were there at the time, and was narrated by a historian.
   (c) An interview with Harold Wilson in 1987 about his time as British Prime Minister in the 1960s.

The line between primary and secondary sources is a rather blurred one. Putting sources into categories is only the first step before asking more important questions like:
— What are the sources evidence *for*?
— How *reliable* are the sources?
— Do they give us a better *understanding*?
— Which sources are the most *useful*?

Often students argue that primary sources 'are more useful to historians than secondary sources because they come from the time of the event'. There are several arguments that support this view.

People who actually lived through or witnessed an event should have a better idea of what happened than people who were *not* there. You might say that film (of whatever kind) and photographs of events taken at the time cannot be in any way 'doctored', so they are bound to give a true picture of events. Official reports or documents, like treaties, are stating what has been agreed, so they cannot be giving a point of view.

Of course, there's some truth in these arguments. But there are other aspects to consider. For example, people who were actually there will not have seen everything which happened. (In any case, they would not have remembered it all!)

They will just have a limited knowledge; they may have been confused or in a state of shock when they made their report. And they will probably want to explain things as *they* saw them.

Film, too, may not be all that reliable. Cameramen are not always allowed to film what they want and, just like anyone else, they cannot witness *everything*.

Official documents pose their own problems. They may only state the final agreement; they may not tell us how that agreement was reached – or what each side thinks of it. Above all, they are often written in quite complicated language.

Students often dismiss secondary sources (especially history textbooks!) as being less valuable than primary sources. They say that, because the writers weren't actually there, they cannot know what happened as well as eyewitnesses can.

On the other hand, people putting together secondary sources have one great advantage. They can study many primary and secondary sources. So their books can give an overview of the whole event from many different viewpoints. Also, writers can present the information in a way suitable for the particular readers. They can choose the right style, or present opposing views.

Exercise

3 You should work on this exercise in groups, using the ideas above and as many of your own ideas as you can. Draw out and complete a chart like that below, and then present it to other groups, explaining your ideas to them.

	Advantages	Disadvantages
Primary sources		
Secondary sources		

3
Subjectivity and Objectivity

So far, you have looked at the different types of evidence available. You have also thought about the different questions which historians try to answer from that evidence.

But sources differ in another important way. Any one source may:
— only give facts about what happened
— only tell you how one individual or group felt about the event
— only give the author's opinion
— only make judgements about people or events.

Of course, most sources give the reader a mixture of fact, opinion and judgement. The reader has the job of sorting them out.

It is important to learn how to judge between these. Otherwise, there is always the danger of accepting one person's opinion as fact. Equally, it is important to use the right kind of source to answer different questions. For example, it will be hard to find out exactly what happened from a personal diary or letter, *or* to find out what people thought about the Locarno treaties by studying the terms of the treaties.

The exercise below, on the Falklands War of 1982, examines these problems.

Exercises

Answer the questions below by studying Sources 3a–3f, under the heading 'The Falklands War, 1982'.
1 Write down which of these sources, if any, is stating:
   (a) facts only
   (b) opinions only
   (c) feelings only
   (d) judgements only.
2 For each of the sources that you have *not* included in your answer to question 1, copy out, under suitable headings:
   (a) those parts that record only facts
   (b) those parts that are giving feelings or opinions
   (c) those parts that are making judgements.

Source 3a
(*Daily Mail*, 5 April 1982. A young sailor on *HMS Invincible*)

We all have mixed feelings about what is going to happen. In some ways, you are looking forward to it but I know my mum was in tears when she heard I was going. It hasn't really sunk in yet but I know I could be going to my death.

Source 3b
(The former British Chief of the Defence Staff said on 4 April)

I think the time for talking is past. I do not think talking is going to do any good now that things have got this far.

Source 3c
(*Daily Mail*, 1 May 1982)

This is still a test of nerve, which may or may not turn into a test of ships and planes. If it does, we can feel confident that the British fleet is as well equipped and manned as it could possibly be. There is probably no better fighting force anywhere in the world.

And in Mrs Thatcher Britain has found the **staunchest** leader anyone could wish. She has made no false move since the crisis began.

The decisive moment is now very close. Success can never be guaranteed but at least everything has been done, and is being done, to deserve it.

Source 3d
(The *Sun*, May 4 1982)

Source 3e
(Colonel 'H' Jones was killed in action at Goose Green in the Falklands. His wife was quoted in the *Daily Express*, 31 May 1982)

We were so proud when we learned how the 2nd Battalion had taken Goose Green and the boys were delighted to see their father hailed as a hero in all the morning papers.

A few hours later, I came home from shopping to find the regimental colonel and his wife in the house, and I knew at once . . .

I just said, 'It's bad news, isn't it – he's dead?' The colonel simply said 'Yes,' and we all broke into tears.

Then I went out into the garden to tell the boys. Rupert burst into tears, but David seemed to take it very well.

Source 3f
(Broadcast by British captain on *HMS Fearless* to Argentinian troops, June 1982)

There is little point in your continuing the struggle. A decision to give up should be made now. This is no reflection on the bravery or skill of your soldiers. However, you are without resupply of ammunition; you have lost considerable quantities of weapons; and we have captured many prisoners. You are unable to prevent these losses continuing.

═══════════════════════

As well as having to identify different forms of information, historians must also be able to test out how *reliable* and *how useful* a source is. Some of the questions a historian might ask of a source are:
(a) Does it tell us all that we need to know, or are there *gaps* in the evidence?
(b) Is the source *consistent*: that is, does one part of it agree with another? Does it give the same version as other sources on the same subject, or does it **contradict** them?
(c) Does it give a particular or *one-sided* view of the subject? Is it **biased**?
(d) Has it *left out* important information that would contradict its point of view?

Exercises 3 to 5 below examine these problems further, continuing the theme of the Falklands War.

═══════════════════════

Exercises
Study Sources 3g–3l below before answering these questions:
3 What do Sources 3g and 3h tell you about most firsthand reports from the Falklands War?
4 List the ways in which Sources 3i and 3j differ in their accounts of the sinking of the Belgrano.
5 Copy out any examples of words or phrases that are biased in sources 3g–3l below.

Source 3g
(Robert Fox, reporting for the BBC, 2 May 1982)

Journalists are not allowed by the Ministry of Defence to comment on what might be happening to other [parts] of the Task Force. 'We don't want to give the Argentines needlessly clues about future movements,' said the senior Royal Navy captain aboard.

The sinking of the Belgrano.

The burial of Royal Marines at Goose Green.

Source 3h
(John Nott, British Defence Secretary, May 1982)

The reports coming from the journalists in the Falkland Islands have generally speaking been magnificent. I have nothing but praise for what the journalists there have done. Of course, we are careful to make sure that no information is released by them that would damage our forces.

Source 3i
(*Daily Express*, 4 May 1982)

An Argentine warship with 700 men on board was 'presumed sunk' last night after being **torpedoed** by a British submarine.

The disaster was announced by the [Argentine] military high command. The 13,000-ton cruiser General Belgrano was blasted by the nuclear-powered submarine Conqueror.

Source 3j
(Brian Hanrahan, reporting for BBC News, 3 May 1982)

At eight o'clock last night a nuclear-powered submarine torpedoed it. It hasn't been sunk, but it has been damaged. The General Belgrano was an old World War II cruiser; it had fifteen big guns and a crew of more than a thousand to man them.

Source 3k
(Lord Carrington, British Foreign Secretary, told the House of Lords, 3 April 1982)

The Falklands are British. Our duty is clear. It is our firm objective to ensure that they are freed from [foreign] occupation.

Source 3l
(*The Sunday Times*, April 4 1982)

Argentina's foreign minister claimed that his country had not invaded any foreign territory but had simply recovered 'part of our national **heritage**.'

The words 'objectivity' and 'subjectivity', used as the title of this chapter, need more explanation. If something is *objective*, it records only the *facts* of what happened and gives no idea of feelings or opinions.

Books like Keesing's *Contemporary Archives* or *An Encyclopaedia of World History* edited by W Langer or the daily reports of the proceedings of Parliament (*Hansard*) are the kinds of sources that are regarded as objective.

This is certainly the case for *Hansard*, which records exactly what was said – even the cheers and boos – by all members of Parliament. (It doesn't of course mean that the speeches the MPs made were objective!)

Langer's Encyclopaedia is not so simple. The editor has to select what facts to include, and which to leave out. In making those decisions, the editor has to judge what is and is not important. This would be like you writing your life story. You would not be able to include everything, or even most things, you have done. In choosing what to include and what to leave out, you will present a particular view of your own life. This situation can be described as 'subjectivity by selection'.

If something is subjective, it might give an opinion or point of view without including any facts or evidence at all. Alternatively, it might *use* the facts or evidence in a particular way. For example, 'Our victory in the Falklands was the greatest since Wellington's at Waterloo' contains some facts, but is a very subjective statement.

It is now possible to link these ideas on subjectivity and objectivity with those on primary and secondary sources in Chapter 2. Historical sources can be placed on two 'scales', one indicating the extent to which it

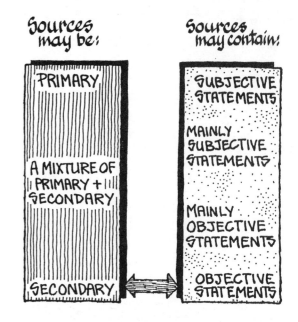

is primary/secondary, the other the extent to which it is objective/subjective.

Perhaps the diagram above will help make this clearer. For instance, suppose we write, 'The Second World War began in September 1939'. That is an *objective* statement; we are not saying what we feel about the event. It is also a *secondary* source because we were not alive at the time. This is shown on the diagram by the arrows.

Subjectivity by selection.

6 Draw the diagram in your book. Take each of the following sources in turn and draw lines to show where you think they fit on the diagram: sources 3b; 3g; 3h; 3i; 3j.

We can now return to the questions originally posed on page 12 that historians ask of their sources:-

1) Are there gaps in the evidence?

Few sources will tell us absolutely everything we want to know about a subject. The problem is to judge how important the gaps are. Are they so great as to make the source useless? Do they mean a particular view comes across? Has there been 'subjectivity by selection'?

2) Are the sources consistent?

Sometimes sources contradict themselves in different places, or are contradicted by other sources. This is more likely to happen with opinions and judgements, but it can happen with facts as well. Here, for example, are three sources commenting on the British landings at San Carlos in the Falklands War:

Source 3m
(C K Macdonald: *Using Evidence*, 1986)

On 21 May 1982 over 1000 British troops went ashore at Port San Carlos in The Falkland Islands. It was the biggest seaborne invasion since D-Day.

Source 3n
(*The Sunday Times*, 23 May 1982)

Dawn, Friday: 2,500 marines and paratroops land unopposed at Port San Carlos.

Source 3o
(The *Sun*, 21 May 1982)

Whitehall chiefs ruled out a huge single operation like D-Day, 1944, with thousands storming on to the beaches. The Defence Ministry said: 'We don't want our boys lying on their bellies and cutting their way through barbed wire **entanglements.**'

Finding differences like this leads historians to investigate further – to check other sources, to look into the background of the authors . . .

If they find contradictions, historians will ask how *reliable* the source is, though they may still find the source *useful*. It still tells them something about the subject, and other sources can be used to find out more.

3) Are the sources biased?

The word bias (and the verb to be biased) literally means 'inclination, **prejudice** or influence', although one-sided is perhaps an easier way of putting it. Often, people make two instant judgements about biased sources:

1 People writing from a particular background are *bound* to be biased. For example, we assume that members of one political party are *always* going to be nice about their colleagues and nasty about the opposition.

Of course, this does happen, but it does not give credit to those people who can make fair and balanced judgements about their opponents. Anyway, we all have opinions, even if some of them are not always visible. So every author is going to be biased in some way.

2 Biased sources are of no use to historians. There is an assumption that, because people are writing only from their own point of view, they are not giving information of any use at all.

Again, this isn't always so. Opinions can be as valuable as facts in giving historians an understanding of the past. Facts alone provide little insight into how people felt about an event. They also give little idea of the reasons why people acted as they did. So if a historian is trying to answer a question that is more than just 'What happened?', a biased source can be extremely valuable.

Exercises

7 Study the set of sources below. They are taken from the party **manifestos** of the Conservative, Labour, Alliance and Scottish National parties, in the 1987 General Election.

(a) State which extract is from which party.

(b) Are these sources all critical of their opponents? Explain your answer by using examples.

(c) Do the sources have any use? Explain your answer.

Source 3p
The choices are between Labour's programme of work for people and Tory policies of waste of people.

Source 3q
The next Conservative Government will build on the achievements of the past eight years with a full programme of positive reform.

Source 3r
All the Opposition parties–Labour, Liberals and SDP–would raise taxation. We believe that it is the wrong thing to do. It will be our aim to do the opposite.

Source 3s
Some Labour-controlled boroughs refuse to co-operate with the police in combating crime. The Conservative Government refuses to recognise that homelessness and unemployment are breeding grounds of delinquency. Both are wrong.

Source 3t
Poverty in Scotland is a tragic twist of fate. In a country rich in so many resources, many of our people live in poverty or on its margins. The British system has failed to solve any of the basic problems of human conditions in Scotland.

Source 3u
Labour's proudest achievement is the creation of the National Health Service. The Conservatives voted against it then. All who use and value the service know only too well how it has been neglected by today's Tories.

Source 3v
We would curb the Tories' divisive policies and stop the destructive antics of the Labour Left.

Two views of the Falklands War. Above: Argentinian magazines showed what they thought of Mrs Thatcher. Below: The *Sun* cartoonist gave his view of the Argentinians.

4
Government and Political Records

The records of all the countries' governments in the twentieth-century form a gigantic store of information for historians. It would be impossible to begin to give details of even a fraction of their contents. As you will see, they are often in obscure language and hard to understand. Nonetheless, it is important that you have an idea of the *kinds* of sources that come under this heading.

Each government keeps a detailed record of everything that is said in its House(s) of Parliament. In Britain, this is called *Hansard*, as it was the name of the printer who first published these details in 1811. Since 1909, verbatim (word for word) reports have been kept, and an extract from these appears below. Similar records are kept for the American Congress, the French Senate and Chamber of Deputies, and the equivalent in other countries. These records provide historians with a complete account of all the debates and arguments that have taken place.

Source 4a
(from Parliamentary Records, 4 February 1976)

Road Sign (Schoolchildren)
Mr. Hall-Davis: Is the Minister aware that there are three different signs to indicate that a motorist may encounter horses and ponies, cattle, or wild animals on the road ahead? It seems that we are rather out of balance in our approach. Should there not be a similar sign indicating that children may be in the road ahead?

Dr. Gilbert: There are signs to indicate the

The House of Commons in session.

presence of schools and that children may be crossing. The hon. Gentleman's suggestion is helpful and constructive and I am hoping to introduce and test provisional signs.

Mr. MacFarquhar: Is my hon. Friend aware that a sign of this type would be welcome in rural Derbyshire, because an increasing number of schoolchildren are having to walk to school in order that their parents can save the increasing bus fares? Will he investigate the operations of the National Bus Company in Derbyshire to ensure that increases in fares, which seem to occur every few months, are genuinely due to rising costs and not to internal inefficiency?

Dr. Gilbert: Naturally we are concerned about the circumstances my hon. Friend has described. He will be aware that the fares that schoolchildren have to pay are partly the responsibility of my right hon. Friend the Secretary of State for Education and Science who, I know, is also concerned about this matter.

Mrs. Knight: Will the Minister bear in mind that there is a particular danger when a stretch of pavement normally in use is out of use because of drainage works or road repairs? Will he look into this aspect of the matter?

Dr. Gilbert: I shall be happy to look at any constructive suggestions for road safety.

Before a Parliament approves a new law, it not only holds a debate, but also often sets up an enquiry to investigate the need for the new law. Governments also use commissions – groups of people including MPs and other experts – to study particular incidents, events or trends.

In America, for instance, the American Congress set up a small group of Congressmen to investigate the Watergate affair that led to the **resignation** of President Nixon in 1974. The reports of all these official enquiries are published and form an important source of detailed information.

The results of the debates and enquiries, in this country, are Acts of Parliament, the laws we have to live by. These laws too provide a valuable source for the historian.

Some government papers and reports, such as the **minutes** of the Cabinet in Britain, are kept secret and not published. The Official Secrets Act allows the government to protect its information from becoming public, normally for thirty years. So, for example, the detailed arguments in the Cabinet during the Suez Crisis of 1956 were only made public at the beginning of 1987.

Source 4b
(When the Cabinet papers of 1956 were made public, a writer in the *News of the World* made these comments, 4 January 1987)

Cabinet papers of Suez times were released last week. Prime Minister Eden personally destroyed a written agreement between Israel, France and Britain.

That was for the three countries jointly to invade Egypt.

Eden and Foreign Secretary Selwyn Lloyd lied repeatedly to the House of Commons. They pretended there was no such agreement.

Exercises
1 Make two lists, one of the advantages and one of the disadvantages of Parliamentary records as sources for historians.
2 Do you think it is right that some aspects of government are kept secret? Explain your answer.

As well as government and political records dealing with the affairs of a particular country, there are many documents dealing with affairs *between* countries.

Some of these are international agreements signed by many countries. The **Covenant** of the League of Nations, drawn up in 1919, is an example of this. Below is Article 16 of the Covenant, which explains what was supposed to happen to any country that attacks another.

Source 4c
(Article 16 of the Covenant of the League of Nations: what this means is explained, line by line, below the source)

'Should any Member of the League resort to war in disregard of its covenants under Articles 12, 13 or 15, it shall *ipso facto* be deemed to have committed an act of war against all other Members of the League, which hereby undertake immediately to subject it to the severance of all trade and financial arrangements, the prohibition of all intercourse between their nationals and the nationals of the covenant-breaking state. . . .'

If a country in the League starts a war
and breaks the League's rules
we shall treat it as if
it had declared war on all
countries in the League. They will
at once take these actions: break off all trade, ban
all relations between their people and
those in the country which has gone to war . . .

18

There are many other international agreements, signed by many countries, covering such matters as the use of the oceans, the treatment of refugees and trading in drugs. Many of these were first drawn up by the League of Nations, and are now the responsibility of the United Nations.

There are also many treaties signed by several countries. For example, the Treaty of Versailles of 1919 was signed by almost all countries involved in the Great War. Many treaties drawn up between the wars, such as the Washington Naval Agreement of 1922 and the treaties of Locarno of 1925, were signed by several countries. Some of these were the countries directly affected by the agreement, such as France and Germany.

Others signed as 'guarantors'. This means that they agreed to 'guarantee' the terms of the agreement. If either side broke the treaty, the guarantors would step in to help the side that had been attacked.

There are also many examples of countries allying with each other. Normally, this means that each agrees to defend the other if it is attacked. At other times, two countries agree to end any disputes between them.

Source 4d is an example of this. It is the full text of the German-Polish Agreement of 26 January 1934. As you can see, it is fairly long, detailed and hard to understand. However, it will give you a flavour of **diplomatic** language, and is connected to other sources later in the chapter.

Source 4d
(The German-Polish Agreement of 1934: A summary of the main points is given below

1 The German Government and the Polish Government consider that the time has come to introduce a new phase in the political relations between Germany and Poland by a direct understanding between State and State. They have, therefore, decided to lay down
5 the principles for the future development of these relations in the present declaration.

The German and Polish Governments think it is time they had a proper agreement.

The two Governments base their action on the fact that the maintenance and guarantee of a lasting peace between their countries is an essential pre-condition for the general peace of Europe.

Peace between Germany and Poland is essential to keep Europe peaceful.

10 They have therefore decided to base their mutual relations on the principles laid down in the Pact of Paris of the 27 August 1928, and propose to define more exactly the application of these principles in so far as the relations between Germany and Poland are concerned.

This agreement is based on an earlier one of 1928.

Each of the two Governments, therefore, lays it down that the
15 international obligations undertaken by it towards a third party do not hinder the peaceful development of their mutual relations, do not conflict with the present declaration, and are not affected by this declaration. They establish, moreover, that this declaration does not extend to those questions which under international law are to be
20 regarded exclusively as the internal concern of one of the two States.

Whatever other agreements Germany and Poland have signed with other countries do not affect this agreement. Nor does this agreement affect home affairs in either country.

Both Governments announce their intention to settle directly all questions of whatever sort which concern their mutual relations.

Should any disputes arise between them and agreement thereon not be reached by direct negotiation, they will in each particular case,
25 on the basis of mutual agreement, seek a solution by other peaceful means, without prejudice to the possibility of applying, if necessary, those methods of procedure in which provision is made for such cases in other agreements in force between them. In no circumstances, however, will they proceed to the application of force for the purpose
30 of reaching a decision in such disputes.

If there is a dispute, they will try and reach agreement through talks. If that fails, they will use other peaceful means.

19

The guarantee of peace created by these principles will facilitate the great task of both Governments of finding a solution for problems of political, economic and social kinds, based on a just and fair adjustment of the interests of both parties.

This guarantees peace between Germany and Poland. This will make it easier to reach agreements through compromise.

35 Both Governments are convinced that the relations between their countries will in this manner develop fruitfully, and will lead to the establishment of a neighbourly relationship which will contribute to the well-being not only of both their countries, but of the other peoples of Europe as well.

Germany and Poland believe this will improve relations between them and help other European countries.

40 The present declaration shall be ratified, and the instruments of ratification shall be exchanged in Warsaw as soon as possible.

Both governments will agree to this treaty as soon as possible.

The declaration is valid for a period of ten years, reckoned from the day of the exchange of the instruments of ratification.

This agreement lasts ten years.

If the declaration is not denounced by one of the two Governments
45 six months before the expiration of this period, it will continue in force, but can then be denounced by either Government at any time on notice of six months being given. Made in duplicate in the German and Polish languages.

If both countries wish, it will continue beyond those ten years. Either Germany or Poland can end it at any time after that, but six months' notice must be given.

Berlin, 26 January 1934

For the German Government:
  FREIHERR von NEURATH.

For the Polish Government:
  JOSEF LIPSKI.

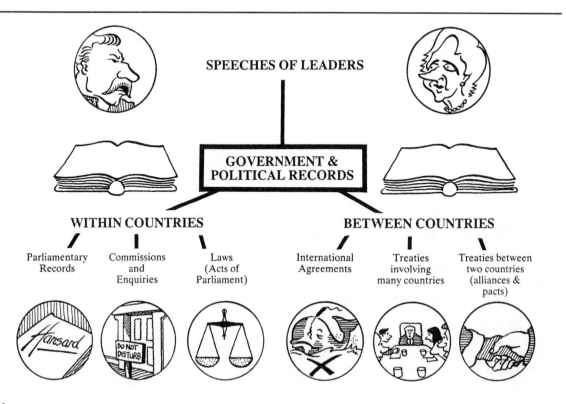

SPEECHES OF LEADERS

GOVERNMENT &
POLITICAL RECORDS

WITHIN COUNTRIES

Parliamentary
Records

Commissions
and
Enquiries

Laws
(Acts of
Parliament)

BETWEEN COUNTRIES

International
Agreements

Treaties
involving
many countries

Treaties between
two countries
(alliances &
pacts)

International agreements of all kinds give the historian detailed information. When examined in conjunction with other documents, they are of great help in answering the question 'What happened when?', thereby forming the narrative of events.

However, in other ways these documents are less helpful. They rarely tell us *why* the leaders signed the agreements. They don't tell us how the decisions were reached. Nor do they give us much idea of what countries actually got in comparison with what they hoped for. They give us little information about the effects of the agreements on the people and countries concerned. And they can be difficult to understand!

The speeches of political leaders are also a valuable source. Some of these are made to the public, others to Parliament. They not only provide information about what happened but can also help to explain the thoughts and ideas of the leader.

Backed up by photographs and newspaper reports, they can also give us an indication of the image the leader is trying to put across. Source 4e below contains some of the views of Hitler on relations between Germany and Poland.

Source 4e

Adolf Hitler, 21 May 1935

The German **Reich** and the present German Government have no other wish than to live on friendly and peaceable terms with all neighbouring States.

Adolf Hitler, 20 February 1938

The Polish State respects the national conditions in [Danzig], and both the city of Danzig and Germany respect Polish rights.

Adolf Hitler, 30 January 1939

During the troubled months of the past year the friendship between Germany and Poland was one of the reassuring factors in the political life of Europe.

Adolf Hitler, 28 April 1939

The German-Polish Agreement resulted in a remarkable lessening of the European tension. Nevertheless, there remained one open question between Germany and Poland, which sooner or later had to be solved – the question of the German city of Danzig. Danzig is a German city and wishes to belong to Germany. On the other hand, this city has contracts with Poland, which were forced upon it by the **dictators** of the Peace of Versailles.

Adolf Hitler, 1 September 1939

I am determined to solve (1) the Danzig question; (2) the question of the Corridor; and (3) to see to it that a change is made in the relationship between Germany and Poland that shall ensure a peaceful **co-existence**. In this I am resolved to continue to fight until either the present Polish Government is willing to bring about this change or until another Polish Government is ready to do so.

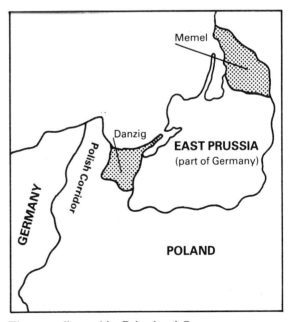

The areas disputed by Poland and Germany.

Source 4f
(Announcement by Herr Forster, Nazi Gauleitér, to the people of Danzig, 1 September 1939).

Men and women of Danzig: The hour for which you have been longing for twenty years has come. This day Danzig has returned to the great German Reich. Our Führer, Adolf Hitler, has freed us.

The Swastika flag is flying today for the first time from the public buildings of Danzig. It also flies from the former Polish buildings, and everywhere in the harbour, the towers of the ancient town hall and St Mary's Church. The bells ring in Danzig's hour of liberation.

We thank our God that He gave the Führer the power and the opportunity of freeing us from the evil of the Versailles [Treaty]. We Danzigers are happy to be able to become citizens of the Reich . . .Long live German Danzig, which has been liberated and returned again to the Reich! Long live our great German fatherland!

STILL HOPE

Punch cartoon of September 1938. Chamberlain flies in search of peace.

Source 4g
(On 2 September 1939 the British Foreign Secretary was sent a telegram by a British official. It contained a statement by M Burckhardt, League of Nations official in Danzig.)

From midnight 30th August until midnight 31st August I was under [watch] of Gestapo agents in Danzig. On 1st September I was visited by Herr Forster. Herr Forster informed me that he considered my [job had ended] . . .If I wished to leave before he did so I had better depart within two hours. During these two hours I was constantly visited by Gestapo agents who tried to [get me to speed up] my departure.

Exercises
Read Sources 4d-4g again.
3 According to lines 23 to 30 of Source 4d, why should Polish people be pleased that their country has signed the agreement with Germany?
4 Study Source 4e.
   (a) At the end of January, 1939, could Polish people still feel **optimistic** that Germany was not likely to attack their country? Explain how you reached your conclusion.
   (b) In April 1939, what did Hitler suggest he planned to do to Danzig?
5 (a) In what ways is Source 4d especially useful to historians?
   (b) What does Source 4d *not* tell you that you would like to know about German-Polish relations?
6 (a) Are Sources 4f and 4g objective statements about events? You should quote from the sources in your answer.
   (b) How does Source 4f support Source 4e?
   (c) Does Source 4f prove that Hitler was correct in saying that Danzig wished to belong to Germany? Explain your answer.
   (d) How could a historian prove that Source 4g was accurate?

22

5
What the Governments Don't Tell You

In the last chapter, we considered the use and value of government documents. But, as the three cases below illustrate, we don't always learn the whole story.

Although many official papers are made public after 30 years, that does not mean the historian can read everything. Some information supplied by spies is still not revealed. And only Government documents are opened up.

Royal Documents

The Royal Family keeps its own documents at Windsor. Only the Queen can decide whether historians can use these. It is quite likely that unknown documents about Nicholas II, the last Tsar of Russia, may still be hidden there.

The same is true of other royal families abroad – and of the **descendants** of former royal families. It is also true in Russia. Historians cannot be sure how many vital details are still kept secret. Nor do they know how many secrets have been deliberately destroyed by governments.

Marilyn Monroe and the Kennedys

In the United States, a special act allows anyone to look at state documents. However, these can still be censored or withheld if the security services think it is necessary.

Marilyn Monroe was a famous American film star who died in 1962. She had taken a drug overdose, although some people believe she was murdered. She was a close friend of the American President, John F Kennedy, and his brother Robert.

The FBI admits it has 31 pages of information filed on her, but it has only released 13 of them. What is in all those other pages? Some of them refer to the Kennedy brothers. Why does the FBI want to keep it secret? No one really knows.

Kennedy's Assassin

In 1963, John F Kennedy was shot dead in Dallas, Texas. A man called Lee Harvey Oswald was arrested for the killing but was himself shot dead soon afterwards.

Was Oswald the murderer? An enquiry, led by Chief Justice Earl Warren, reported in 1964. Yes, said the report, Oswald was the killer, and he had done it entirely on his own.

But not everyone agrees. Some historians believe that some evidence is missing. Others believe that Warren was wrong. Kennedy was certainly murdered but perhaps the real murderer got away.

Exercises

1 a) Suggest reasons why (a) the Royal Family and (b) governments might want to keep something secret.
   b) Why do you think official papers are not made public *at once*?

2 Does this mean it is impossible ever to find out the truth about an event? Explain your answer.

6
Personal Documents

The title 'personal documents' includes a variety of different sources. The four most important are shown opposite.

This form of evidence is most valuable in helping historians to understand people. It can give them an idea of a person's character, ideas and beliefs. It can help them to see why people acted as they did, and took the decisions that they did. It can also show them how people were affected by events.

On the other hand, personal evidence is bound to have its limitations. It is likely that it will present an event from only one point of view, so there is a danger of it being subjective or biased.

For example, a **kulak** keeping a record of his or her experiences in Stalin's Russia will give a later generation an excellent insight into what it was like to live through those times. But the kulak is unlikely to have known much about the experiences of others in different areas. Nor will he or she have much understanding or sympathy for Stalin's policies or the reasons for them.

Personal documents can also be very disappointing. Historians expect them to be full of detail and excitement. Yet they are often very day-to-day, and tell us little. Here, for example, is a letter that Joseph Stalin wrote to his daughter on 8 August, 1939. (He called her his 'little housekeeper'.) At that time Russia was holding important talks with both Britain and Germany about a possible alliance. A non-aggression pact between Russia and Germany was signed just fifteen days later.

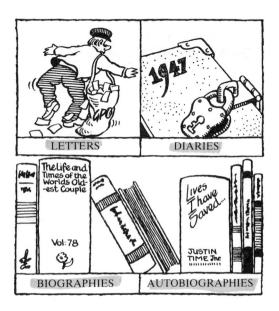

LETTERS   DIARIES

BIOGRAPHIES   AUTOBIOGRAPHIES

Source 6a

Hello, my little Housekeeper!

I got both your letters. I'm glad you haven't forgotten your little Papa. I couldn't answer you at once. I was busy.

I hear you weren't alone at Ritsa and that you had a young man with you. Well, there's nothing wrong with that. Ritsa is nice, especially if you have a young man with you, my little sparrow.

When do you mean to set out for Moscow? Isn't it time? I think so. Come to Moscow by 25 August, or even the 20th. Write me what you think of this. I don't expect to come south this year. I'm busy. I can't get away. My health? I'm well. My spirits are good. I miss you a bit, but you'll be coming soon.

I give you a big hug, my little sparrow.

Diaries and Letters

Historians must work out the value of these sources before they know how to use them. So they must ask questions about each diary or letter.

1 Why was it written? If it was written so that it could be published later on, it may keep a careful record of events. But many letters and diaries are scribbled down quickly to keep a note of appointments, to pass on information or to record thoughts, feelings or events in the writer's personal life. So a historian wants to know both the *purpose* of writing it and the *circumstances* in which it was written.

2 To whom was the letter addressed? Some letters are just personal, sent to a friend or relative. Others are addressed to a newspaper, and intended for a wider readership. The author will probably have written the letter with a particular *audience* in mind.

3 What was the author's view of himself or herself? Whatever it was, it will affect how useful the document is. Some people are determined (or can't stop themselves!) to make themselves look the 'hero of the story'. Others try to be more objective, and give credit to other people for the part they played.

4 How much did the author know about the event(s) he or she has written about? Some people will have played a major role; perhaps they helped make key decisions. But others just stood on the sidelines or may only have been slightly affected.

The exercise below explores these questions by examining three letters about the Tsar of Russia, Nicholas II.

Exercises
Study the sources below, and then answer the questions that follow them.

Source 6b
(C A Almedingen of the Imperial Navy described to his aunt a lunch he attended at the Winter Palace, 1907)

We had no idea the Tsar was in St Petersburg. We had just sat down to a most magnificent spread when he came in unannounced. I dropped my napkin and my neighbour his fork. We all leapt to our feet. He told us to sit down and took his own place at one of the tables. We noticed that he ate very little and drank no wine.

Then he made the rounds of all the tables,

The Tsar and his advisers.

26

telling us to remain seated even when he spoke to any of us. Quite apart from his being a Tsar, we all felt that he was a warm-hearted, simple and hospitable man. He spoke little and seemed to say so much, and he remembered names, too, of those who had fallen at Tsushima.

I do wish many more people could get to know him as he is and could have seen him just like that. At the end there came such a homely detail: he told us to take all the fruit and the sweets to our 'sisters' and 'those others – you know what I mean.' Never had I imagined the Tsar could be so simple. I am sure nobody would hate him if they knew him.

Source 6c
(Tsar Nicholas II to his wife)

Mogilev, 7 September 1915
My Beloved Sunny,
My warmest thanks for your dear letter, in which you spoke of your visits to the refugees in various parts of the town! What an excellent idea, and how splendid that you should have been and seen everything for yourself!

Yesterday, although it was Sunday, was a very busy day. At 10 o'clock, church; from 11 to 12.30, work on the Staff, a big lunch, then Scherbatov's report (Minister of the Interior); I told him everything. A half-hour's walk in the garden. From 6 to 7.30, Polivanov's report in the presence of Alexeiev, and after dinner his private report, and then, a mass of beastly papers for signature . . .

I . . . would give a great deal to be able to nestle in our comfortable old bed; my field bedstead is so hard and stiff! But I must not complain – how many sleep on damp grass and mud!

God bless you, my love, and the children! Tenderly and passionately I kiss you times without number.
Ever your old hubby,
Nicky.

Source 6d
(Tsarina Alexandra to her husband)

Tsarskoje Selo, 11 November 1916
Beloved Sweetheart,
Forgive me, deary, believe me – I **entreat** you don't go and change Protopopov now, he will be alright, give him the chance to get the food supply matter into his hands. Oh, Lovy, you can trust me. I may not be clever enough – but I have a strong feeling and that helps more than the brain often. Don't change anybody until we meet, I entreat you, let's speak it over quietly together.

You don't know how hard it is now – so much to live through and such hatred of the rotten upper sets. The food supply must be in Protopopov's hands. Others are **intriguing** against him, he heard the news from the Headquarters some days ago. Times are serious – don't break up all at once.

Goodbye, my Angel. Once more, remember that for your reign, Baby and us you need the strength, prayers and advice of our Friend [Rasputin]. Remember how last year all were against you . . . and our Friend gave you the help and strength you took over all and saved Russia – we no longer went back. Protopopov **venerates** our Friend and will be blessed. Quieten me, promise, forgive, but it's for you and Baby I fight.
Kisses yours,
Wify.

SOURCE	PURPOSE & CIRCUMSTANCES When and where was it written? And why?	AUDIENCE Who was the letter for?	What view does the author give of him or herself?	INFORMATION What does the source particularly tell us about?	INADEQUACIES What does the source especially *fail* to tell us about?
6b					
6c					
6d					

1 Using the whole page, draw out and fill in a chart like that on page 27.

2 Using the ideas and information on your chart, write a summary explaining how *useful* and *reliable* you consider each of Sources 6b, 6c and 6d to be.

Diaries

On 6 June 1944, Allied troops landed on the Normandy beaches. Here is what two people wrote in their diary that day:

Source 6e

(This lady was German and living in Berlin. Her husband, Hugo, had a good job in the Nazi party).

6 June
Went out around midday – saw groups of people in the street. I thought there had been an accident, but it was far far worse. The English and Americans have invaded France.

Hugo's cousin had a telegram about the same time – I saw the boy delivering it as my neighbours were telling me the news and my heart nearly *stopped* – it was bad news for him, not me. He had his leave cancelled and had to return to Russia.

Hugo and his friends talked until after midnight. They say it is the beginning of the end. The enemy have superiority on air, sea and land. What will happen? What will happen to us?

Source 6f

(Anne Frank was nearly 15. She was living in hiding in Amsterdam because she was Jewish.)

Tuesday, 6 June, 1944
'This is D-day,' came the announcement over the British Radio and quite rightly, 'This is *the* day.' The invasion has begun! . . .

According to the German news, British parachute troops have landed on the French coast. British landing craft are in battle with the German Navy, says the BBC.

We discussed it over breakfast at nine o'clock: Is this just a trial landing like Dieppe two years ago?

British broadcast in German, Dutch, French, and other languages at 10 o'clock: 'The invasion has begun!' – that means the 'real' invasion. British broadcast in German at 11 o'clock, speech by the Supreme Commander, General Dwight Eisenhower . . .

Great commotion in [their hideaway]! Would the long-awaited liberation that has been talked of so much, but which still seems *too* wonderful, *too* much like a fairy-tale, ever come true? Could we be granted victory this year, 1944? . . .

The best part of the invasion is that I have the feeling that friends are approaching. We have been oppressed by those terrible Germans for so long, they have had their knives so at our throats, that the thought of friends and delivery fills us with confidence!

Now it doesn't concern the Jews any more; no, it concerns Holland and all occupied Europe. Perhaps, Margot says, I may yet be able to go back to school in September or October.

[Note: In August, their hideaway was discovered and they were arrested. Anne Frank died in Belsen concentration camp three months before her sixteenth birthday.]

Exercises
3 On what fact do both writers agree?
4 (a) What is the attitude of each writer to the event? Give two examples from each source to show what you mean.
  (b) Why do the writers have different views?
5 (a) Are these primary or secondary sources? Give a reason.
  (b) Is this firsthand or secondhand information? Explain your answer carefully.
  (c) Why should each writer treat the sources *she* has used with care?
6 How do the writers' opinions about the effects of this event differ?
7 Which source would be most useful to a historian? Explain how you decided.
8 Apart from diaries, what sources could a historian use to find out about German attitudes to D-Day?

Autobiographies

When important people write the story of their lives, the autobiographies that result will be of great value to historians. They will probably include far more details of events than more general books. They will have stories and comments about other people who played a part in events.

As a result, historians will be able to gain a better understanding of the motives of people and of the discussions that went on. The different points of view of those involved will be identified. In the end, a more detailed and accurate picture of why things happened as they did is likely to emerge.

On the other hand, autobiographies must be treated with caution. It is quite often the case that they are not always written by the actual people. (Modern sports stars are not the first to use ghost writers.) The story in the box below illustrates an especially famous case of this. Even if the subjects have written their own stories, it may be that they were written deliberately to show off their part in events. (Although we must be careful not to assume that *all* autobiographies are written for this purpose and will necessarily be biased.)

We do not always know whether the authors were in a position to know everything that happened. It may be that they had access only to some information.

In 1914, an American firm published *My Own Story* by the **Suffragette** leader, Mrs Pankhurst. A recent reprint calls it '*The Autobiography of Emmeline Pankhurst*'. But, in a way, it isn't!

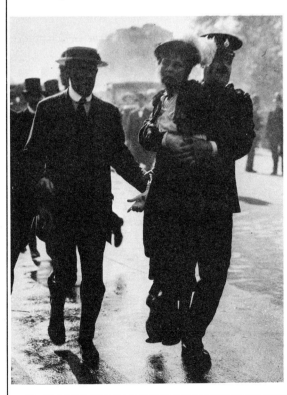

Andrew Rosen, a modern American historian wrote:

Mrs Pankhurst never really wrote an autobiography. *My Own Story* [was mainly] the work of Rheta Childe Dorr, an American journalist who, according to Sylvia Pankhurst, produced the book 'from talks with Mrs Pankhurst and from Suffragette literature'. It is so [full of] errors and glossings-over as to be [almost] useless to the historian.

Another modern writer, Jill Craigie, wrote in 1979:

Dorr boarded the ship with [Mrs Pankhurst] on 11 October 1913. For two weeks on her journeys, and on odd days free during the tour, the journalist had Mrs Pankhurst all to herself. The dictation began on the first day of the journey to New York.

In other words, Mrs Pankhurst did not write her own story. She told it to someone else – and the other person wrote it down. So it is oral history, rather than an autobiography.

But Ms Craigie disagrees with Mr Rosen about its value:

True, there are several errors, but the 'glossings-over' are no more numerous or misleading than those common to most **memoirs**.

In the exercise that follows, you are going to read a short autobiography by Benito Mussolini, first published in the *Sunday Express* on 8 December 1935. On 24 July 1943 when Mussolini was dismissed as Prime Minister of Italy, the *Daily Express* reprinted the article.

THE KIND OF MAN I AM

By BENITO MUSSOLINI

ON December 8, 1935, the Sunday Express published an article by Mussolini himself, analysing his own character.

The headline to the article was as above.

The Daily Express republishes this illuminating document today. The brave words of 1935 have a vital interest on this historic day when Mussolini stands exposed before the world.

AS a soldier in the world war I was in my element, and felt nothing in that rôle to clash with my Socialistic tenets.

For the stout trench-fighter—and I was a model in that respect—learns stark lessons in the "class" conflict. Besides, blind obedience to life-or-death orders can render a man fit for high command. It is a stern school, with memories that helped me later in my march on Rome.

War is, in truth, the supreme moral training for a man's nerves and will.

Another weapon I discovered early was the power of the printed word to sway souls to me.

Machiavelli

The newspaper was soon my gun, my flag—a thing with a soul that could mirror my own.

I had browsed early on Machiavelli's writings. My blacksmith father used to read the great Florentine aloud to us at night as we sat beside the dying embers of the forge, drinking our peasant wine.

The impression then made upon my young mind was profound and lasting. And when again I read Machiavelli for myself at the age of 40, his book acted on me with extraordinary force.

Then Bismarck's power allured me. I thought him the greatest political realist of his century.

As for Napoleon, he was never a paragon of mine, since our activities differ entirely. He wound up a revolution. I never even commenced one.

As First Consul he shone out as a great man, but with the Empire his decadence began; and Beethoven's fine instinct was right to withdraw the famous Dedication to the "Eroica" Symphony. For the crown seemed always to impel Napoleon towards new wars.

But for all that, I contend there *can* be imperialism without any empire. That is not necessary, since the faster such empire spreads, the more it must fritter its cohesion and organic strength.

But the "imperialistic" urge is quite distinct, an elementary force of our human nature, like the will-to-power itself.

Thus we see the imperialism of Dollardom, we have it also in the religious and artistic spheres.

And in each and every guise it is symptomatic of man's quenchless vitality.

No sooner is one born than the "imperialist" within presses his claim—in the nursery, at school, and in every sport. That clamorous force ceases only with death itself.

Consider great Cæsar's career. He has always fascinated me as a commanding giant among men—one who united in his powerful soul the warrior's will and the prescient genius of a prophet-philosopher.

But at bottom Cæsar contemplated all things *sub specie æternitatis.*

Aye, he loved glory indeed. Yet his pride forbade him to share it with humanity at large.

Love—and Fear

HERE I am reminded that men have asked me, "Can a dictator be ever *loved?*"

My answer is:—

"He can—when the masses at the same time fear him."

For the crowd will always love *strong* men; in that respect the mob resembles a woman.

In me the soldier instinct lives always; the call to duty *as I alone see it.* The rest is with fate.

When I was in command in Milan I received the King's telegram bidding me to take over the governing power.

Was I astonished? Or did I *expect* that triumph.

I expected it!

I have also been asked to make clear my own soul-state during that momentous journey to Rome, and all that it meant to me . . . and to others besides!

As I remember it, the question ran like this: "Did you feel like an artist embarking on his own work, or, rather, like a prophet carrying out some high mission?"

I am immortal

I am as clear now as to the tumult of that hour as I was in that Romeward express.

I was the artist, summoned to a commission that was to make me immortal.

Yet always I was ready to return to a hut from any palace. But once arrived in Rome from Milan, some potent magic took hold of me with strange webs of thought.

In the dusk I would walk around the grand gardens of the Villa Torlonia—where now I live.

And the fact of owning a fine horse to ride seemed too great a marvel to believe in my changed life.

Yet soon I adapted myself to new sumpturay laws. I ate less; chiefly fruit and vegetables.

I drank less wine, avoided social distractions, and spent night as well as day at a desk that chained me inexorably.

Each hour seemed split into a hundred duty-particles. A frenzy of labour, you may will it: the passion of a martyr, or else of a man condemned to death and therefore "making his soul," as we say, before meeting him judging God.

This, then, is I: I could do no other then, and never can so long as I live.

Swaying the people

Perhaps it is something of this potent "me" that sways the people.

I am told I have wondrous sway in this respect. It may be so, and is a gift that carries heavy responsibility.

Certainly the masses cast their spell upon me as a shoal of fish tempts the fastidious angler, or man with a capacious net.

Enthusiasm and interest are my two lines in this tireless play. If I use one item only, then I run a risk of loss. Reciprocal charm must swing between us.

It is so different with the printed word or the witchery of radio broadcasts. Those reach millions in silence.

But the seas of human faces upturned to me on my vast piazza!

Those tense uplifted hearts, those bright, eager eyes—and thunderous voices like the crash of storm-surf on a rocky coast!

It is the *ear* that takes fire in such cases as these from my torrents of words. An eternal marvel to me, as also to them!

My aim is twofold with an audience: to clarify my central theme and at the same to suggest some new thing.

How well I know the crowd for these thirty-odd years!

There must needs be a *festal* element in the music I give them; the high Roman salute, the lilt of song with kindling memories, and pathos.

After all, it is only faith that can shake the mountains! A mystical instrument. The masses have little time to think. And how incredible is the willingness of modern men to believe!

King-fish!

When I feel I have the crowd in my hand they seem plastic as clay to me. Then I am the king-fish of the shoal!

But, strangely enough, I at the same time experience a sort of aversion, like that of the poet against the craggy word-stuff he works in. A sense of exasperated disappointment I would call it, as the sculptor so often feels when his marble falls short of the first ecstatic vision he has conceived of it.

But, somehow, I can console myself when all is over, for all my success depends upon my dominating these ductile masses *as an artist!*

Some critics may call me inconsistent. I disagree with Winston Churchill, who calls the gigantic army of France a guarantee of peace.

And yet I will put guns (they say) into the hands of little babes! True enough. But I claim to educate and fortify those innocent children for the new lottery of our Italian life. We are so different from the rest of you! And for so many reasons!

They tell me, also, that "Pride" is seen running through the whole warp and woof of my public life.

It may be so.

I define Pride as "the high consciousness of oneself."

Vastly different from this, I hold, are Hauteur and Arrogance: those I would style the degeneration of true Pride, which can be a magnificent, all-conquering trait. Now, ask me of what I am proudest in my whole career, and I reply unhesitatingly: *To have been a good soldier in battle.* For *that* must needs give a man proof of his own soul-strength—the quality which the old Greeks besought of their gods instead of mere fugitive, temporal favours.

My childhood

As a child long ago in a wretched village home, my own early pride suffered bitter humiliation; schooling, as well as my daily bread, was of the "third class."

It is such ordeals as those that make a man "revolutionary." But character and circumstance control us inexorably. And love of country is a passion best measured by the size of our sacrifice.

I never lost faith in my star from the moment the call came to me in that theatre-box in Milan.

Then I was all for *action!!* Anything like sitting still, the frittering of life's precious hours and sheer immobility—that is to me like the torment of damnation.

Let me speak here without any fetters. I am all for *movement.* I must be for ever marching onward. Aye, and *upward,* too—as in the stormy mountain trail with the vast panorama beneath me widening gloriously as I go. That is it: exulting in my *own* Alpine chain!

For private friendship I have no genius at all.

We become strong, I feel, when we have no friends upon whom to lean, or to look to for moral stay or guidance.

Such is my temperament, as well as my estimate of men.

A friend can prove an enemy.

In that case I grapple with him; otherwise I can have no nexus or interest in any man.

Each day I receive many people of many conditions of life and rank. Well, I say I simply "receive" these.

Yet, somehow, they are far away from me; even here sitting in the big fauteuils before my desk in this noble, historic hall, my visitors remain dim and remote from my innermost self.

They speak. I answer them. But always I remain completely alone.

'Live dangerously'

Some of my foreign callers seek to interpret my personality to the world outside. But how can this be done with accuracy after only a brief and random talk? They may even come primed with significant sayings or writings of my own.

One of these was: "I long to make a masterwork of my life!"

Another: "I would like to *dramatise* my career—I mean in the larger and nobler sense of that word, drama." Or yet again, they will recall to me how I adopted Nietzsche's "reckless" motto: "Live *dangerously.*"

And then I am asked how so proud and "hidden" a nature as my own could at the same time claim that my supreme aim and goal was my people's interest. I reply to this that the people's welfare and future greatness is in itself a supremely *dramatic* thing.

So the more I concentrate all my energies upon *that*—the more devotedly I serve it—so is my own insignificant life magnified into fierce glowing. Herein is my religion. I see it shining steadfast unto glory!

I care little

For my own personal safety I care little—as all Rome can see, and as all Italy knows.

A thousand police may be on watch around me. I may be urged to sleep every night in a different place. All these precautions do not move or touch me.

I move freely abroad as I please—on horseback, in a motor, or on my racing cycle. If I gave even a moment's thought to my body's security humiliation would follow, and a sense of shame of which I can say I am not capable.

Dark things have been said of me. I have little to say in reply.

Except *this.* I am no demi-god, but just a man of courage, never afraid to stalk out into the light and battle for his own soul-felt convictions.

If I have erred, it is only because I am human. I also have my strong loves and my hates, my deep sorrows and simple joys.

I am a man who lives on his nerves; a solitary soul driven on by destiny and craving ultimate repose and peace.

So my silence must defend me from calumny. But to one great sin I shall here confess: **"I have loved my Italy with an idolatrous love!"**

FLASHBACKS

"I know, don't tell me! Three seconds later a thousand-pounder fell on the very spot where you'd been standing!"

"You stoppa da grumbling! If it hadn't been for me you'd never have hadda da Empire to lose."

"Nice, Corsica, Tunis, Savoy!!! . . . Sorry, everybody . . . Omit Tunis!"

Exercises

9 What does Mussolini tell you in this article about:
   (a) his family and early life?
   (b) his personal life after he became leader?
   (c) his attitude to friendship with others?

10 Which of the following words or phrases seem, from your reading of this article, to apply to Mussolini? In each case, explain why you chose the ones you did and why you rejected the others.
   — brave
   — thoughtful
   — someone who has a high opinion of himself
   — cautious
   — someone who dislikes war and fighting
   — patriotic
   — a man of action
   — a man who considers all the possibilities before deciding what to do.

11 Does this autobiographical article:
   (a) provide a lot of information about events that took place?
   (b) tell you what it would have been like to live in Mussolini's Italy?
   (c) give you information about Mussolini's character?
   In each case, explain your answer.

12 How *useful* and *reliable* would you regard this as a historical source?

Biographies

Biographies will have many of the same advantages as autobiographies. The authors will have researched their subjects carefully. They will have studied as many of the available documents and papers, including diaries and letters, as possible. They will have interviewed many people who knew the subject and, if possible, will have spent hours with the subjects themselves.

The biographies that result will give a very full picture of those people. So, like autobiographies, they will be an invaluable source, helping historians to answer not only the question 'What happened?' but also 'Why did it happen?' and 'What did people think and feel about it?'

However, biographies too will have their disadvantages. The authors may not have been able, for a variety of reasons, to get at all the information. They may wish to portray their subjects in a particularly favourable or unfavourable light. The resulting books can therefore be biased.

Authors will obviously want people to buy their books so they try to make their stories more interesting and appealing. To do this they might have to leave out some details, or make some things sound a bit more exciting than they really were.

You may well be able to find several biographies that give a different view of the same person. Some twentieth-century leaders, like Hitler, have been condemned by nearly everybody. But others, like Stalin and Mussolini, have had defenders as well as critics. Others again, like Winston Churchill, Charles de Gaulle or President Kennedy, whom we might expect to have been praised, have been criticised by some historians.

In the exercises that follow, you will be examining a variety of opinions about Joseph Stalin, ruler of Russia from 1928 to 1953.

Exercises
Study the sources that follow before answering the questions on page 32.

Source 6g
(*The Penguin Political Dictionary*, 1942)

Trotsky has described him as the **traitor** of the revolution, while others continue to see in him the unswerving leader of world **Communism**. Stalin's **regime** has been marked by a distinct rise of [Russia] as a Great Power, by economic and **cultural** development of Russia. But Communism [has not succeeded] as an international movement. Stalin's role for Russia has been compared to that of Peter the Great [a former tsar], whom he personally admires.

Source 6h: An idealised portrait of Stalin

Source 6i
(*Comrade Stalin – Leader of Progressive Mankind*, a pamphlet written in 1950)

The peoples of the Soviet Union look upon Comrade Stalin as their recognized leader and teacher. Today they express their warm love and devotion to Comrade Stalin and acknowledge his great services in the struggle for a happy life and for peace among nations.

The eyes of the people of the Soviet Union and of hundreds of millions in all countries turn with deep gratitude to Comrade Stalin, the beloved leader and teacher.

Source 6j
(Nikita Khrushchev, Soviet leader, speaking in 1956)

Stalin showed in a whole series of cases his intolerance, his brutality and his abuse of power. He often chose [to have killed] not only enemies, but also individuals who had not committed any crimes against the Party and the Soviet Government.

Source 6k
(*The Sunday Times*, date unknown)

By 1929 he held undisputed power. Then, at immense cost, within a decade Stalin made Russia an industrial nation. This enabled her to withstand Hitler's attack in 1941, and to recover from [the war] to become the world's second greatest industrial power.

Source 6l
(from a Moscow radio announcement when Stalin died in March 1953)

The life of the wise leader and teacher of the Communist Party and Soviet people, Lenin's comrade and brilliant disciple, J V Stalin, is over.

Source 6m
(from an American book, 1973)

At the height of his power, the Russian press showed Joseph Stalin as the humble son of poor parents, modest, kindly, and fond of children. The Western press was more likely to describe him as an **arrogant**, insensitive, power-hungry Communist czar.

Stalin was determined to modernize Russia at all costs. In this he succeeded. He was tough and shrewd and callous, an ideal combination for climbing to the top amid a shrewd, callous, cut-throat crowd.

13   Identify:
  (a) which of the sources gives a favourable impression of Stalin.
  (b) which of the sources gives an unfavourable impression of Stalin.
  In each case, quote at least one phrase that helped you to make your decision.
14   Which of the sources gives a *balanced* view of Stalin, pointing out both the advantages and the disadvantages of his rule? Explain your answer by reference to the source.
15   How is it possible for different authors to hold such different views of the same person?

32

7
Newspapers

Newspapers are a rich source of information for historians. The editorial content can help to answer many of the questions that historians pose.

Not only can newspapers help in this way, but also, through their advertisements, letters, television and radio programme lists and many other aspects, newspapers can begin to give a later generation an idea of what life was like at a particular time.

What happened?

Why did it happen?
What were the effects?

What did people think
and feel about it?

Exercises

1 Look at the cigarette advertisement from the *Picture Post*, 3 May 1941 on page 34. List at least two things it tells you about people and cigarettes at that time.

2 Find and cut out any modern cigarette advert. Stick it into your book, and write a short comparison between the modern advert and the 1941 one.

3 Study the other advertisement, taken from the same 1941 magazine.
  (a) Why do you think it has chosen to use this story?
  (b) Do you think it will have helped to increase sales? Give reasons for your answers.

du MAURIER

THE FILTER TIP WILL KEEP YOU FIT

IT IS NOW MORE THAN EVER NECESSARY TO EMPTY YOUR PACKET AT THE TIME OF PURCHASE AND LEAVE IT WITH THE TOBACCONIST

NORMA KNIGHT wants you to meet . . .

Mrs. Brown who has organized a gardening corps

All my neighbours have gardens and . . .

1 . . as our menfolk have joined up we women decided to carry on with the gardening and produce lots of vegetables.

2 We found that digging wasn't hard work if we were all doing it together, so now we have what we call "digging parties."

The kindly luxurious lather of Knight's Castile soothes away that feeling of exhaustion after hard work, tones up the skin and keeps the complexion youthfully clear.

3 Then we go home to tea and a good wash with Knight's Castile. We all use Knight's Castile because it's marvellously soothing after a hard day's work.

Knight's Castile

PREVENTS 'TIRED SKIN'

KC 285-760 · · · JOHN KNIGHT LIMITED—SOAP MAKERS SINCE 1810

Two advertisements from *Picture Post*, 3 May 1941.

4 Choose any subject of national or international importance, for example, nuclear weapons, events in one of the world's troublespots or a topic like world hunger. For one week, make a collection of newspaper cuttings about your topic. Try to do this using two different papers. At the end of the week, put your collection together. Then use your sources to write a summary account (of about 250 words) of what has happened that week. Finally, explain in what ways your two sources *differed* in their coverage of the topic.

5 This could be done as a group exercise, and could be in the form of a comparison between two or more present day papers, or between one modern and one older paper. Analyse each of the different types of information included, such as
— national news
— international news
— letters
— editorial comments
— sport
— financial news
— TV and radio news
— photographs
— advertisements
You should do this by counting up how many column inches are devoted to each category. Then draw up charts or diagrams to illustrate the different types. Finally, write a report on your findings, and evaluate the paper(s) you have studied.

Daily Mirror
EUROPE'S BIGGEST DAILY SALE
5p   Thursday, October 10, 1974   No. 21,996

We said it in February. Now we say it again

Daily Mirror
EUROPE'S BIGGEST DAILY SALE

FOR ALL OUR TOMORROWS
VOTE LABOUR TODAY

THE WAY AHEAD; Turn to Page Two

Although they can be of great value, newspapers must be treated with great care. Imagine what view of late twentieth-century Britain future historians might get if their only source was a year's supply of just one daily paper.

Newspapers in most countries support a political party. They want to show that party in a good light. This will be most obvious at election times, as the front page from the *Daily Mirror*, above, illustrates. But at other times they will include editorial comments that favour one party, and may report events in a subjective way. This may have become obvious to you as you worked on Exercise 4 or 5. You can see other examples on page 38. But newspapers sometimes change their views, as these two sources show.

Source 7a
(*The Sun* **editorial** of 10 October 1974)

Perhaps there has never been an Election when it was harder to make up one's mind fairly. But make up our minds we must. That is what **democracy** is all about.

The Sun makes this pledge: Whatever happens today this newspaper will back ANY Government in ANY measures, however unpopular, which we judge to be in Britain's best interests.

Source 7b
(*The Sun*, 4 October 1986)

The Sun has decided to let the Conservative Party into a little secret.

We know when the next General Election will be held.

So Tories, get your diaries out and put down MAY 1988.

What's more we also know who is going to win: Margaret Thatcher.

The Tories will win because Labour will be forced to fight the election as the party that promises to RAISE taxes. What a slogan!

Let's have a ringing declaration that Maggie's revolution goes on. That there will be MORE trade union reform – the voters love it.

Newspapers are keen to make sure they sell more copies than their rivals. So they will try to pick on stories that they think will appeal to the kind of people who read their paper. They will also try to report news in an exciting and even exaggerated way.

Often, many of the news items will not be very important at all. They will be there only to attract readers. Here, for example, are the headlines from *The Sun* on 9 August 1974, and from the *Morning Star* of 4 October 1986. Which do you think was which?

PENSIONER FIGHTS FOR FREE TV LICENCE

RACIST CRICKET CIRCUS

JUDGE WON'T BUDGE

US LIBYA LIE EXPOSED

THREE-DEATH INQUEST TOLD OF LOVE AFFAIRS

ICE GIRLS IN HOT WATER

HOW THE KIDS BEAT MUM AT BEDTIME

'VAMPIRE' TRIAL

35

One major problem with using newspapers is trying to judge what value to place on an article, both as a source of information and as a guide to opinions at the time. (The exercises on pages 34 and 35 illustrate this.)

In some cases, reporters will write stories that come across as factual accounts, but actually contain their own opinions. At other times, reporters will quote from eyewitnesses. Yet such people may well be in a state of shock, and may not have seen the whole of an event. Even then, reporters will have to cut down their interviews to just a few lines, and will pick what to use and what to leave out.

During times of crisis, newspapers are even more fascinating, but also dangerous, sources. The press during the British General Strike of 1926, when each side produced its own paper, is an excellent and easily available example of this.

Papers are often **censored** at these times with the editors only being allowed to publish what the government says they can, so there are sometimes blank sections. In South Africa, the papers have been censored at the same time as being forbidden to leave blank spaces!

The question of censorship becomes even more difficult during wartime. Governments are anxious to tell people what is happening. But at the same time they do not want people to be disheartened by bad news. Nor do they want to give away information that could be of use to their enemies. As a result, reporters are given strict guidelines about what to report. Their stories are then reviewed by censors.

There are also cases in which the newspapers censor themselves. This was especially the case in the 1930s, in what has become known as the **Abdication** crisis.

Edward, Prince of Wales, first met Mrs Simpson in 1930. Over the next few years, they became first friends and then fell in love. In 1935, Mrs Simpson went on holiday with the Prince to Austria.

George V died in January 1936 and Edward became king. His friendship with Mrs Simpson continued. He went on holiday with her that summer. But the British press reported none of it. The newspaper owners reached a gentlemen's agreement *not* to publish anything about the relationship. This 'pact' lasted until 3 December 1936.

Only one publication broke the silence.* A weekly magazine published a photo of the two together on holiday. But its caption said: 'The Duke of Lancaster and a Guest'. Foreign papers *did* run the story.

Source 7c
The *New York Daily News* commented:

Most [British publishers] think of themselves as **statesmen** first and publishers second, a long way second. They feel they must mould public opinion through their papers by telling the public only what the public should hear.

The Prince of Wales and Mrs Simpson.

*Notes
1   British readers *could* have learned about it if they subscribed to American journals – or through the Communist magazine *The Week*. But this was distributed by post.
2   The last time that private royal affairs had been mentioned in the press was in the 1890s when a sporting magazine headed its news column with an (apparently) irrelevant headline:
NOTHING WHATEVER BETWEEN THE PRINCE OF WALES AND LILY LANGTRY
The following week's column was headed:
NOT EVEN A SHEET

Exercises
6   What do you think are the particular
    (a) advantages and
    (b) disadvantages of newspapers as historical sources?
7   How can newspaper reporters get their own opinions into stories that they write?
8   Why do you think the South African government made it illegal for newspapers to leave sections blank?
9   Why did British newspapers in the 1930s keep quiet about Edward and Mrs Simpson?

Newspaper reports of the Angolan Civil War

1 Background information

Angola is a central African country that used to belong to Portugal. In the early 1970s, the Portuguese gave their African colonies independence. Three different groups then fought each other for control of the government of Angola. They were:
— UNITA, led by Jonas Savimbi. They were keen to make sure Angola did not become Communist, and fought against . . .
— the MPLA, led by Agostinho Neto. This was a leftwing group, which received help from Communist countries.
— The FNLA, led by Holden Roberto, was the third group. They wanted a rightwing government, and were supported by the United States. Roberto had been paid by the American CIA (Central Intelligence Agency) for 14 years.

2 The American reporters' briefing

Before going to Angola, American reporters were given a 'briefing' by the CIA. The purpose of this was to give them background knowledge about the war, and tell them the American government's view.

John Stockwell, who had been CIA Commander for Angola, described what happened:

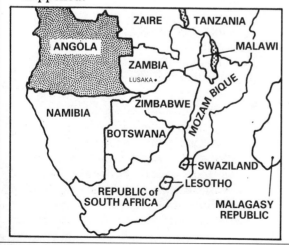

The first briefings on Angola went literally, 'Gentlemen, this is a map of Africa. Here is Angola.' And then they went on to describe that there were three **liberation** movements – 'one of them is led by Holden Roberto. He's the good guy. Then, the MPLA is headed by this drunken Marxist poet, Agostinho Neto. He's the bad guy.'

The basic theme was to make it look like Russian and Cuban **aggression** in Angola. So any kind of story that you could write and get into the **media** anywhere that pushed that line, you did. One third of my staff was **propagandist**. Their career jobs were making up stories and finding ways to get them into the press.

3 The reports from Angola about Russian advisers

John Stockwell commented on one story as follows:

Our man in Lusaka [the capital of neighbouring Zambia] ran a story that the city of Melanje had been captured by UNITA forces and, in doing so, they captured 20 Russian advisers. They thought this would show that Russians were running the thing in Angola. It wasn't a fact and we knew that.

Fred Bridgeland worked for Reuters news agency in Angola. His job was to write reports that would then appear in American and British newspapers. This was what he said later about the capture of the 20 Russian 'advisers':

'I remember reporting that very clearly. I pinned it on an official UNITA **communique**. Years later, I discovered that a little CIA **misinformation** expert had sat in the US Embassy in Lusaka and composed that communique and it bore no relationship to truth.

I had absolutely no idea [whether it was true]. You've got to remember, during a war, you're working under incredible pressure. I worked for four months without a day off for 16 hours a day. All that was wanted was a flow of information. With hindsight, from the side I was reporting, most of the official statements were completely false.'

4 The reports of 'the Cuban rapists' in Angola

Another account John Stockwell gave was this:

He [the CIA man in Lusaka] came up with another story which kept going for weeks. It was a good story, in terms of the CIA's propaganda interests. He had some Cuban soldiers raping some young Angolan girls, then there was a battle and he had that Cuban unit cut off and captured. And then he had the Cubans' women victims identifying their rapists. And then there was a trial and they were convicted. Then he had them executed by a firing squad of the women who had been supposedly violated, with photographs of young African women with weapons shooting down these Cubans.

There had never been a rape. There had never been a military action. The Cubans had never been captured. It was all fiction. All the information we were getting was that the Cubans were handling themselves brilliantly, and very generously towards the Africans.

The report below appeared in the *Daily Express* in Britain on 12 March 1976.

LUSAKA, Thursday.—Women guerrillas in Angola are reported to have executed 17 Cuban soldiers for crimes of "rape and murder."

A message from the nationalist movement UNITA said the Cubans were shot after being tried by a "people's tribunal."

Five of the 17 had been identified as members of a group of Cuban troops—who support the Marxist Government—who raped four black women, aged 15 to 22, at a village near Huambo.

On trial

A firing squad comprised entirely of women was formed and the Cubans were shot with their own guns. The Angolan Government denies the executions took place.

Meanwhile the new Angolan Government is to put a British mercenary named Baker on trial.

Baker—his first name is not known—was captured last month as he tried to escape from Angola by swimming across the River Zaire.

An Angolan officer is reported to have said : "The mercenary will be given a trial. That is the law."

5 In conclusion

John Stockwell said:

We had set ourselves well above and beyond the law, beyond the Congress, beyond the Constitution. We were lying to the President, lying to the Secretary of State, lying to the Congress about what we were doing.

Fred Bridgeland concluded:

Basically, you can publish any old [rubbish] you like and it will get newspaper room . . . I would say people are very silly if they believe everything that the newspapers tell them and I think probably anybody who buys a newspaper needs a course on how to read newspapers.

Exercises

10 (a) What view of events, according to Stockwell, did the CIA hope that reporters would give?

(b) How reliable a source of information do you think Stockwell is?

11 Given the reports in Sections 3 and 4, did the CIA achieve its aims? Explain your answer.

12 Study the *Daily Express* article opposite.

(a) Are there any words or phrases in it that show bias? If so, explain what they are saying. If not, does this make the report reliable?

(b) Do you think British people reading this report would have any reasons to doubt its truth? Explain your answer.

13 Do you agree with Fred Bridgeland's conclusion? If not, explain *why* not. If you do, what do you think should be included in a 'course on how to read newspapers'?

8
Cartoons

Cartoons are always entertaining, and this makes them an attractive way of presenting history. Their impact also helps us to remember things that might otherwise soon be forgotten. Most of us enjoy comic strips when we are young, and cartoons seem to be an extension of these.

They make our usually serious leaders look rather silly, and exaggerate their funniest characteristics. A classic example of this is shown above – the gigantic nose of the French leader Charles de Gaulle. The photograph opposite shows how big it really was.

However, cartoons are far from easy to use as historical sources. They certainly don't tell us very much about what happened, as that is not their purpose. Also, you often need to know quite a lot about an event in order to understand the point of the cartoon. Look at the cartoon on the left of page 41, taken from the *Daily Telegraph* of 1978.

Above: French leader de Gaulle blocks Britain's entry to the EEC—by using his nose! Below: de Gaulle in person. Nose apart, how accurately did the cartoonist draw him?

To understand it, you need to know:
1 that it is a take-off of the famous British First World War recruiting poster which had the same title;
2 that the man is Fidel Castro, leader of Cuba, who is famous for his big beard, smoking cigars and wearing an army cap;
3 that his beard has been made into a map of Africa, with countries named on it where Cuban troops went in the 1970s.

So the point the cartoonist is making is that Castro is interfering in Africa by sending Cubans to fight there. But without a lot of background knowledge, it would be hard to understand.

With background understanding, cartoons can give a good insight into a particular point of view. Usually, this is the cartoonist's own idea, though sometimes it is the view of the newspaper for whom the cartoonist is working. Here are two famous examples:

Will Dyson's cartoon 'Curious! I seem to hear a child weeping.' appeared in 1919. It shows the Big Four leaving the Paris Peace Conference after drawing up the treaty of Versailles. It became such a famous cartoon because it predicted almost exactly what was

PEACE AND FUTURE CANNON FODDER

The Tiger: "Curious! I seem to hear a child weeping!"

to happen. The children who had grown up by 1940 were indeed to be weeping, because they were to fight a Second Great War.

'The price of petrol' cartoon by Zec appeared in the *Daily Mirror* on 6 March 1942 when petrol was scarce because of German attacks on tankers. The Government was furious. They thought it meant that petrol companies were making huge profits while sailors were dying. Zec explained that he was trying to warn people not to waste fuel.

41

Exercises

On this page are four cartoons from 1963. Each makes a comment about the Nuclear Test Ban Treaty signed that year by the leaders of the USA (President Kennedy), the USSR (Mr Khrushchev) and Great Britain (Prime Minister Macmillan). These three are shown, right to left, in the British cartoon. The only other countries with nuclear weapons – France and China – refused to sign. Study the cartoons carefully, and then answer these questions as fully as possible.

1 Who are shown sitting on the branches of the tree in the German cartoon?
2 In the British cartoon, what are the leaders going on to build if their paper boat floats?
3 The Japanese cartoon is suggesting that the nuclear weapons are just on the surface; what lies under them?
4 Who is the person in the American cartoon meant to be?
5 Do you think the cartoonists are all pleased and optimistic about the signing of the treaty? Explain your answer fully.

U.K. "Trial launching." Papas in the *Guardian*.

Germany. "Insel der Glückseligkeit." Hicks in *Die Welt*.

U.S. "Is it a mirage?" Justus in the *Minneapolis Star*.

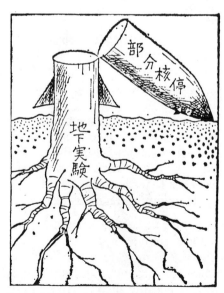

Japan. "Eradicate the roots too, please." Tsuchida in *Sankei*.

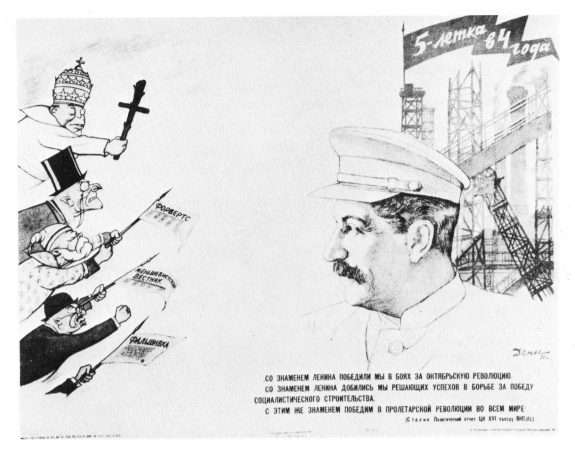

СО ЗНАМЕНЕМ ЛЕНИНА ПОБЕДИЛИ МЫ В БОЯХ ЗА ОКТЯБРЬСКУЮ РЕВОЛЮЦИЮ.
СО ЗНАМЕНЕМ ЛЕНИНА ДОБИЛИСЬ МЫ РЕШАЮЩИХ УСПЕХОВ В БОРЬБЕ ЗА ПОБЕДУ СОЦИАЛИСТИЧЕСКОГО СТРОИТЕЛЬСТВА.
С ЭТИМ ЖЕ ЗНАМЕНЕМ ПОБЕДИМ В ПРОЛЕТАРСКОЙ РЕВОЛЮЦИИ ВО ВСЕМ МИРЕ.

(Сталин. Политический отчет ЦК XVI съезду ВКП(б).)

It is not only newspapers which publish cartoons. Very often, governments use them to get across a particular point or even to advertise what they have achieved. In the Second World War, the British government issued many in the 'Careless Talk' series to discourage people from talking about things that might be helpful to the enemy.

you never know who's listening!

CARELESS TALK COSTS LIVES

Above is an example of a **propaganda** poster from the Soviet Union in the 1930s. On the right is Stalin, standing in front of the achievements of the Five Year Plans. On the left are the enemies of the Communist State – the Church, **capitalists**, the elderly and foreigners.

Exercise

6 Draw a line down the centre of a page. Head one half 'The value of cartoons as historical evidence' and the other half 'The problems of using cartoons'. Then write down as many things as you can under each column. Try to include references to the cartoons in this chapter as you do so. Here are two to help you start – you have to choose which column to put them in.

— They are often amusing and easy to remember, for example De Gaulle's nose, Castro's beard and cigar.

— They are sometimes just propaganda, like the ones the Russians produced in the 1930s.

9
Visual Evidence

The title 'visual evidence' usually covers forms of evidence which include little or no writing, although they may have a **commentary.**

This chapter concentrates on photographs and recorded film. However, many of the points made also apply to the other forms of visual evidence, such as drawings, paintings and 'live' television broadcasts.

Photographs

By the early years of this century, cameras had been in use for some time. So for all the major events of this century, there is a huge stock of photographic evidence. There are photos of leading people in all kinds of situations, of soldiers in battle, of hospitals and schools, of sporting occasions, of famine and flood . . .

These photographs can be helpful in giving historians a better idea of what events were like. It is hard to imagine the full horror of trenches in the First World War without some pictures to help. Exercise 1 below is designed to help you test this out.

Exercises

1 This is an exercise to be done in pairs. One person should just read Sources 9a and 9b. The other should just study Source 9c, the photograph that appears on page 45. Neither should study the other's evidence. Each should then write down what they can learn from their sources.

Then they should compare their findings and, together, write an answer to the question: How helpful are photographs as evidence?

Source 9a
Adrian Stokes fought as a lieutenant in the Battle of Loos in 1915, when he was aged 16. In 1981, he recalled his feelings:

My men relied on me, I was kept very busy; so when people ask me, 'what did it feel like to be a boy of sixteen in France?', I answer that I seldom had time to think of tomorrow. If I had been a private things could have been very different.

Of course, I knew fear; who didn't? . . . In the trenches, when waiting for the signal to clamber out and get going, my fear became more about losing [my men's] respect, than about all the ghastly things that must happen any minute now. I thank the seniors for drumming that into me. If I had been a private things could have been different.

Source 9b
Frederic Manning was a private, who fought on the Somme in 1916. In 1930, he published *Her Privates We*; it was a true account of his experiences, although the characters were made up. An attack is about to begin . . .

Bourne's fit of shakiness increased, until he set his teeth to prevent them chattering in his head. Fear poisoned the very blood. He heard men breathing irregularly behind him, as he breathed himself; he heard them licking their lips, trying to moisten their mouths; he heard them swallow, as though overcoming a difficulty in swallowing; and the sense that others suffered equally or more than himself, quietened him.

Some men moaned, or even sobbed a little, as though they struggled to throw off an intolerable burden of oppression.

Bourne shifted his weight on to his other foot, and felt the relaxed knee trembling. It was the cold. If only they had something to do, it might be better. It had been a help simply to place a ladder in position . . .

'It'll soon be over, now,' whispered Martlow.

Good luck, chum. Good luck. Good luck.

He felt his heart thumping at first. And then, almost surprised at the lack of effort which it needed, he moved towards the ladder . . .

Source 9c

2 (a) How long after the event was Source 9a written?
  (b) Why should a historian treat this source with care?
  (c) Frederic Manning *invented* the characters in Source 9b. Does this make the source useless to a historian? Explain your answer.

Photographs can also be helpful in illustrating the things and people that we read about. For example, pictures of **technological** achievements begin to give us an idea of the meaning of what we read about.

Equally, it is hard to read about twentieth-century leaders without having, at least in our minds' eyes, a picture of them. However, many leaders have been very careful about which pictures of them were shown, as you will see later.

Photographs of ordinary people can help us to better understand their feelings. The question 'What did people think and feel about events?' is sometimes better answered by a photo. The photograph below, of a soldier carrying the wrapped and labelled remains of his baby son in the Vietnam War, illustrates this.

However, the use of photographs as historical evidence has many problems.

We have just noted how photographs help us to understand other people's feelings and thoughts. Look at the photograph above of a man looking very pleased with himself, his dog and his car.

Is he the manager of a team that's just won promotion? A pop star's manager? A pools winner? In fact, it would be almost impossible for anyone to guess! He is a Pole. The car was, in 1984, the only 3.5 litre Rover in Poland. He runs a jewellery business and is a millionaire in a Communist country. Could anyone have worked that out from the photo?

Photographs are not very helpful for telling us what happened. Nor can a single photograph ever give us a full impression of an event. It is almost certain that the photographer will have only seen one part of an event and may well have only got a view from a distance. Then a newspaper editor may well select which of the photographer's pictures to use to suit a purpose.

For example, the photograph here is of Hitler arriving in Linz in 1938. The crowds are cheering, and it certainly seems as if the **Anschluss** was popular. Yet compare the impression that photograph gives with Source 9d.

Source 9d
(*Berlin Diary* by William Shirer, published in 1941)

Vienna, 22 March 1938
Tess's condition still critical. [Tess was his wife and she was in hospital.] And the atmosphere in the hospital has not helped. First, Tess says, there was a Jewish lady whose brother-in-law committed suicide the day Hitler entered town. She screamed all the first night. To-day she left in black mourning clothes and veil, clutching her baby.

On the streets to-day gangs of Jews, with jeering **storm-troopers** standing over them and taunting crowds around them, on their hands and knees scrubbing signs off the sidewalks. Many Jews killing themselves. All sorts of reports of Nazi **sadism**. Jewish men *and* women made to clean **latrines**. Hundreds of them just picked at random off the streets to clean the toilets of the Nazi boys. The lucky ones get off with merely cleaning cars – the thousands of automobiles which have been stolen from the Jews and 'enemies' of the regime.

One picture which Hitler did not want the public to see. This 1939 shot showed him wearing glasses. So the negative was cancelled with a cross.

===

Exercise
3 (a) Do you think the crowd is pleased to see Hitler or not? Explain how you decided.
   (b) Does this prove that all Viennese people were pleased (read Source 9d)? Give reasons.
   (c) What does this tell you about photographs as evidence?

===

   There is an old saying that 'the camera cannot lie'. Historians have good reason to doubt this. Politicians are always eager to create a good impression. They often use photographs to help them do this. They are photographed with children, or workers, or whoever, to show that they particularly care for that group. They make sure any photos that create the wrong impression are *not* published. They even have photographs altered to ensure the correct image is conveyed.

Not quite the image Stalin wanted. Notice the pock-marks; photographs of Stalin had these removed before publication in Russia.

Creating an image: Benito Mussolini was always keen to use photographs to help his image. Though he was short, clever camera angles were used to make the jump look higher. The pose with the violin was also designed to impress people.

Changing the image: these two photographs show the first Communist President of Czechoslovakia, Gottwald, signing new agricultural laws in 1948. In the original photo, on the left, several members of another political party, the Social Democrats, were shown. The official version shows only the President and the Minister of Justice, another Communist. (Many similar examples are available from Soviet Russia, especially during the time of Stalin's rule.)

Exercises

4 In this chapter, several of the problems of using photographs have been examined.
   (a) What do you consider the three main disadvantages of photos as historical evidence are?
   (b) Given these disadvantages, are photos of *any* value as historical evidence? Explain your answer.

5 You will need to use other sources to do this exercise. Research photographs of one or more twentieth-century leaders in text books, magazines etc. If possible, take copies of them. Prepare and mount a display which includes a commentary on the way in which leaders have used photography to their advantage or disadvantage.

Films and television

The information explosion of the twentieth-century has been most dramatic in the field of film, television and video. You have probably seen film of soldiers in the First World War. They were taken from a distance, and are usually seen running in a rather jerky fashion. Compare that in your mind with some of the television film you can see today: detailed close-ups, instant replays, split screens – all are commonplace.

It is important to distinguish between different forms of film. Documentaries and news broadcasts are designed to pass on illustrated information about events. They are therefore helpful in providing information, which is often more easily understood than, say, radio news, or written news.

Remember though that not all the film that was shot will be shown. Editors will have chosen what they want to be shown. So the problem of subjectivity by selection (see page 14) will arise. An example of this is described in Source 9e below. Also, a commentary will have been written and added.

Source 9e

In May 1985, there were riots at a football match in Brussels and 38 people were crushed to death when a wall collapsed. *The Sunday Times* interviewed Stephen Claypole, who worked for BBC News, about its coverage of the event.

Claypole told the story of a BBC cameraman working in Brussels on the night of the European Cup final. He was by the wall that collapsed in the Heysel stadium: 'He filmed for a full 15 minutes and we had the whole thing in London in under two hours.'

But, Claypole added, 'Nothing was used. You can't show a child slowly dying, or a policeman trying to open somebody's windpipe with a truncheon.'

Documentary film has, throughout the twentieth century, been used by governments as propaganda. Here are three examples of this.

In 1934, Adolf Hitler asked the film director, Leni Riefenstahl, to make a record of the Nazi Congress at Nuremberg. The film that resulted was called *Triumph of the Will*. After opening titles, it begins with these words on screen (in four separate titles):
— on 5 September 1934
— 20 years after the outbreak of war
— 16 years after the beginning of German suffering
— 19 months after the beginning of Germany's rebirth

It also includes the words: 'The Party is Hitler, but Hitler is Germany, just as Germany is Hitler!' Hitler himself said: 'On the one hand I want to use the film fully and completely as a medium of propaganda, but in such a way that every viewer knows that today he is going to a political film.'

George Perry, a film critic, said the film was 'dangerous, brilliant and appalling; it can induce ecstatic response in its audience, and consequently should be viewed very objectively.' Today, *Triumph of the Will* is rarely shown. It is illegal to show it publicly in East and West Germany.

After 1938, every German film programme began with a newsreel, which opened with a fanfare and a shot of a national symbol, the German eagle.

Exercises
6   In the opening sequences of *Triumph of the Will*, what events were referred to as 'the beginning of German suffering' and 'the beginning of Germany's rebirth'?
7   In the 1960s, the director Leni Riefenstahl said, 'Everything is real. And there is no commentary. It is history. A purely historical film.' Do you agree with her? Explain your answer.
8   Why do you think it is illegal to show *Triumph of the Will* in Germany?

Scene from *Triumph of the Will*.

Hitler with Leni Riefenstahl.

Communist Russia also made use of film. Their best known producer was Sergei Eisenstein. In 1930, he said: 'With us, 'art' is not a mere word. We look upon it as only one of many instruments *used in the class struggle.*'

It was seen as a way of showing Russian people how the working class, led by their heroic Communist leaders, had overcome the wealthy ruling classes. His films were documentaries that *re*-created history. They often filmed in the original places. But they also added pieces. For example, in the picture below, from *Battleship Potemkin*, troops representing the ruling class are seen firing on ordinary people. In the original **mutiny** of 1905, which the film was supposed to show, that never happened.

The 'Odessa Steps' sequence from *Battleship Potemkin*

50

We should not assume that only dictatorships use film in this way. Here is the commentary from a famous Second World War British documentary, *London Can Take it*.

LONDON CAN TAKE IT!

I am speaking from London. It is late afternoon and the people of London are preparing for the night. Everyone is anxious to get home before darkness falls, before our nightly visitors arrive.

Now, it's eight o'clock. Gerry's a little bit late tonight. The searchlights are in position. The guns are ready. The people's army of volunteers is ready. They are the ones who are really fighting this war – the firemen, the air raid wardens, the ambulance drivers.

And there's the wail of the **banshee**. The nightly siege of London has begun. The city is dressed for battle . . . Here they come . . . Now the searchlights are poking long white inquisitive fingers into the blackness of the night . . .

These are not Hollywood sound effects. This is the music they play every night in London. The symphony of war . . . [sequence omitted]

Sooner or later, the dawn will come. The German bombers are creatures of the night. They melt away before the dawn and scurry back to the safety of their own airdromes. And there's the wail of the banshee again, this time a friendly wail. The all-clear signal tells us that the bombers

have gone. It's just six a.m. In this last hour of precious sleep, this strange new world finds peace.

London raises her head, shakes the debris of the night from her hair and takes stock of the damage done. London has been hurt during the night. The sign of a great fighter in the ring is: can he get up from the floor after being knocked down? London does this every morning. [sequence omitted]

Dr Goebbels said recently that the nightly air raids have had a terrific effect upon the **morale** of the people of London. The good doctor is absolutely right. Today the morale of the people is higher than ever before. They are fused together not by fear, but by a surging spirit of courage, the like of which the world has never known. They know that thousands of them will die but they would rather stand up and face death than kneel down and face the kind of existence the conqueror would impose upon them. And they know, too, that . . . England is not taking its beating lying down. They are guarding the frontiers of freedom. [sequence omitted]

I am a **neutral** reporter. I have watched the people of London live and die ever since death in its most ghastly **garb** began to come here as a nightly visitor five weeks ago. I have watched them stand by their homes. I have seen them made homeless. I have seen them moved to new homes and I can assure you – there is no panic, no fear, no despair in London Town. There is nothing but determination, confidence and high courage among the people of Churchill's island. [sequence omitted]

It is true that the Nazis will be over again tomorrow night, and the night after that, and every night. They will drop thousands of bombs and they'll destroy hundreds of buildings and they'll kill thousands of people. But a bomb has its limitations. It can only destroy buildings and kill people. It cannot kill the unconquerable spirit and courage of the people of London.

London can take it!

You will see that film, like any other form of historical evidence, needs to be used very carefully. For every piece of film, the historian must ask many questions:
— Does it contradict or support other forms of evidence?
— Was it made for a special reason (such as propaganda)?
— Under what conditions was the film made?
— Was it shot 'live' (as the event happened) or was it a later reconstruction?
— Was the director able to film everything he or she wished?
— What was missed out?
— Above all, which questions can the film help to answer?

Exercises
You will need to study Sources 9f and 9g to answer these questions.
9 Source 9f is taken from Eisenstein's film *October*. It shows the events of 1917, and was made in 1927. In this still, the actor playing Lenin, Nikandrov, is seen arriving at Finland Station. How accurate a picture of the real event do you think this is? Explain your answer.
10 Source 9g is the commentary used on a newsreel showing the Italian attack on Abyssinia in 1935. The section between the stars was censored for British audiences. In what way does leaving this part out change the report? Why do you think this was done?
11 In the extract from *London Can Take It* on page 51, the commentator says, 'I am a neutral reporter.' Does his commentary give that impression? Explain your answer.

Source 9f: From 'October'.

Source 9g
To Mussolini goes warning that the League of Nations will **invoke** penalties against him if he does not [stop] his war of conquest★ ★ ★ . Soon the full strength of His Majesty's Home Fleet is steaming down towards the Mediterranean. The penalties will be economic first, but British troops follow the fleet to Malta and Egypt. There is even talk of closing the Suez Canal★ ★ ★ . Mussolini is unmoved by the British warning. Into Africa he keeps pouring his **legions** and, at the appointed hour, hurls them forward against the Ethiopian vastnesses, unconquered even by the Caesars. Stirred by Mussolini's war, the British electorate, marching to the polls in a General Election, strongly **endorses** its government's stand for strong League action.

10
Statistics

Statistics can provide some of the 'hard' evidence that other sources lack. While letters or photographs help us to understand how people thought or felt about an event, statistics can tell us what was actually happening.

There is a large variety of different kinds of statistics. Some of those you are likely to come across include:

(a) Statistics about aspects of the economy of a country. It is hard to judge what is happening in a country without some figures to help. The graph below shows unemployment in the United States during the Depression. Note that the figures are presented as a percentage, rather than in millions of people. Why do you think this is?

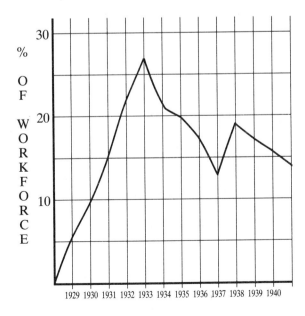

(b) Election results. Historians of the twentieth century are often concerned with politics, so political statistics can be of great help. Here is a summary of British General Election results from 1931 to 1987.

General Election	Conservative	Liberal	Labour
1931	471	72	65
1935	387	54	166
1945	189	25	396
1950	298	9	315
1951	320	6	296
1955	344	6	277
1959	365	6	258
1964	303	9	317
1966	253	12	363
1970	330	6	287
1974 (Feb)	296	14	301
1974 (Oct)	276	13	319
1979	339	11	268
1983	397	23	209
1987	375	22	229

Note: 1983 & 1987 Liberal figures include SDP members.

(c) Population statistics. These may simply provide information about the number of people in a country. However, they can be more detailed, giving details by age, sex, racial origin etc. United Nations statistics about the populations of the United States and Russia from 1965 to 1980 are shown on page 54.

USA	Units	1965	1975	1980
Population	million	194.3	213.6	222.8
Density	infants per sq mile	54	60	62
Annual population growth	%	1.3	1.0	1.0
Infant mortality	per 1,000 live births	24.7	16.1	14.0
Life expectancy	years	69	71	73
Urban population	%	68	70	73
Illiteracy	%	n.a	1	1
Education:				
primary & secondary	%	100	100	100
higher	%	40.2	58.2	56.0
TV receivers	‰	362	571	623
Radio receivers	‰	1,235	1,882	2,048
Navy	'000	867	733	708
Air Force	'000	829	612	563
Army	'000	963	785	751
Military expenditure	% GDP	7.6	6.0	5.2

USSR	Units	1965	1975	1980
Population	million	230.9	254.5	265.5
Density	infants per sq mile	26	28	31
Annual population growth	%	1.2	0.9	0.8
Infant mortality	per 1,000 live births	27.2	27.8	0
Life expectancy	years	68	70	70
Urban population	%	51	61	65
Illiteracy	%	n.a	1	n.a.
Education:				
primary & secondary	%	95	89	90
higher	%	29.5	22.1	21.6
TV receivers	‰	68	217	890
Radio receivers	‰	320	481	n.a.
Navy	'000	450	500	433
Air Force	'000	510	400	475
Army	'000	2,000	1,825	1,825
Military expenditure	% GDP	(12.8)	(10.3)	(9.4)

Exercises

1   Draw graphs to compare the information on the USA and USSR for
    (a) total population
    (b) higher education
    (c) television sets.
    Make sure that you use suitable scales for each graph, and that you use different colours for the two countries.

2   What conclusions can you draw from comparing the information for the two countries?

3   For what purposes are statistics an especially useful form of evidence?

Like other forms of evidence, statistics must be treated with care. It is especially important to consider how the statistics were collected. In some cases, such as most election results, the figures cannot be doubted. However, economic statistics are less easy to collect.

Think about figures showing a country's coal production. To start with, production figures have to be given from every single coal-mine. There may be hundreds of these. And think of the problems at each of these mines:

— How can we be sure that the coal has been weighed accurately?
— Does *all* coal count – or only coal of a certain quality?
— If the government wants output to go up, will the miners admit to low figures?

As well as asking *how* the statistics were collected, we need to find out *why*. Often, the government simply wants to know what is happening. But sometimes they are keen to show how well they are doing, compared to the previous government or another country.

Background information

In 1928, Stalin introduced the system of Five Year Plans to Russia. The idea was to improve the production of industrial goods as rapidly as possible. The government in Moscow decided how much each industry was to produce. Targets were then set for each industry, and, within it, each factory.

Source 10a summarises Stalin's view of the achievements of the First Plan. Source 10b shows how much was produced in 1927, what the plans *hoped* to achieve, and what was *actually* produced as a result of the First Five Year Plan (1928–32) and the Second Five Year Plan (1932–37). Sources 10c and 10d give some insights into *how* these things were achieved.

Source 10a

The **fundamental** task of the five-year plan was to transfer our country, with its backward technology, on to the lines of modern technology.

The fundamental task was to convert the USSR from an **agrarian** and weak country, dependent upon the **caprices** of the capitalist countries, into an industrial and powerful country . . .

We did not have an iron and steel industry, the basis for the industrialization of the country. Now we have one.

We did not have a tractor industry. Now we have one.

We did not have a machine tool industry. Now we have one.

We did not have a big modern chemical industry. Now we have one.

We did not have a real and big industry for the production of modern agricultural machinery. Now we have one.

We did not have an aircraft industry. Now we have one.

In output of electric power we were last on the list. Now we rank among the first.

In output of oil products and coal we were last on the list. Now we rank among the first . .

It is true that we are 6 per cent short of fulfilling the total programme . .

It is true that the output of goods for mass consumption was less than the amount required . .

Source 10b

(Industrial Production – in millions of tonnes)

	1927 Production	1932–33 Planned	1932–33 Actual	1937 Planned	1937 Actual
Coal	35.4	68.0	64.3	152.5	138.6
Oil	11.7	22.0	21.4	46.8	28.5
Steel	4.0	8.3	5.9	17.0	17.7

Source 10c

(In his book *Russia*, published in 1940, Bernard Pares describes what happened to Professor Vyacheslav Chernavin during the Plans)

Take the published case of Vyacheslav Chernavin who was known to me before the Revolution. He was no politician – perhaps he may have been a Liberal. He was put in charge of the fishery service in the White Sea and told to bring about an enormous increase of the catch; he asked for the necessary trawlers, but never got them: he was asked to confess to deliberate 'wrecking'; he refused; he was imprisoned, so was his wife; he was told that if he confessed, he would get a light sentence and she would be set free, if not, both would be kept prisoner. Both refused to give way, so he was sent as a convict to the Arctics, though still in charge of the fisheries: from there, with his wife and their small boy, he escaped into Finland.

Source 10d
(In his book *I Search for Truth in Russia*, published in 1936, Sir Walter Citrine, a British trade union leader, describes a part of his visit to a bearing factory)

Then we went through the works and one of the first things which struck me was that every now and again there was a large brown painted board on which in white chalk were marked up the names of workmen and percentages against these. I was introduced to the foreman, a Russian-American. He told me that these figures represented the increased percentage of previous output that the workers had undertaken to produce during the current year. They were all employed on piece work and after last year's output they were asked to produce still more. They undertook to produce the figures stated against each man's name, namely, 125 per cent of the previous year, or 150 per cent, as the case might be. The board showed against this the actual result and whether a man was lagging behind or not. I immediately asked what about the man who was failing to increase his output. What happened to him?

The foreman replied, 'We do not put up any black lists or anything like that'.

Reassured by this, I went along and soon after came across a larger board. It was ruled with columns down the left-hand side and was ruled also horizontally. In the left-hand column starting from the top there was a picture of an aeroplane. Next below it there was a motor-car. Next below it some other figure **emblematical** of speed and so on, the figures representing a lower and lower speed of movement. One was of a man riding a mule. Another showed a man walking leisurely; another a tortoise; another a snail, until at the bottom there was the figure of a man lying fast asleep. Against some of these lower sketches were written names and percentages.

I said to the foreman, 'What is this? You told me you didn't put up a black list, but what is this?'

Exercises
4   Refer to Source 10b.
    (a) Draw a graph to illustrate the *actual* figures of production, 1927–1937. Label one axis 'Millions of tonnes' and the other 'Years'. Use different colours for each industry. In the appropriate colour, mark with a star the *planned* production for each industry in the years given.
    (b) Did any of the industries at any time do better than planned?
    (c) Which industry, at which time, had the greatest shortfall? Explain how you decided.
5   Refer to Sources 10a and 10b.
    (a) Does Stalin present an optimistic or a **pessimistic** view of the Five Year Plan? Explain, using quotes from the source, how you decided.
    (b) Do you think Stalin's view is fair?
    (c) Study the following figures of grain production:

    Grain harvest (in millions of tonnes)
1928	1930	1932	1934	1935
74.8	85.2	91.0	69.0	76.5

    Do these alter the view of the Five Year Plans you have gained from Sources 10a and 10b? If so, how?
6   Refer to Sources 10c and 10d. What do these sources tell you about *how* the increases in production were achieved?
    (a) Copy and complete each of the following *in as much detail* as you can, referring to the sources for examples: Statistics are especially helpful in telling us about. . . . However, they give us little information about. . . .
    (b) Is there any sign of bias in any of these sources? If so, give examples.

11
Oral History

'Oral' literally means 'spoken'. So oral history is the name given to the history that is spoken by people talking about their experiences of historical events. It is an increasingly popular form of history. It gives many people the chance to be a historian, by recording what they are told, and thus adding to the total sum of historical knowledge. It also gives others a chance to tell us what they know and feel about events in their lifetime.

This can be a very helpful form of history for learning how ordinary people were affected by national or world events. In contrast, textbooks usually only give an overall view of what happened. Secondly, people can provide details of local events that might otherwise be eventually lost. In addition, an individual talking can give an immediacy and a vividness to events.

On the other hand, we all know that our memories are far from perfect. We are liable to forget things and to confuse details. This is especially the case if people are being asked to talk about things that happened a long time ago.

Sometimes, several people talking about the same period or event will have different views of it. So it may be that a combination of several different people's views will be needed.

Setting up an oral history assignment

An oral history assignment can be an interesting way of completing a GCSE coursework assignment. Some of the stages that you will need to go through are outlined here.

Choosing a topic
Try to ensure that the subject you choose is not too wide, like 'Experiences of the Second World War'. At the same time, it should not be too narrow or limited, like 'Memories of Askerswell Youth Club in 1953'.

COME ON, GRAN, YOU MUST KNOW THE PRICE OF BEEFBURGERS IN 1902...

Finding people to interview
Try to make sure your subjects are willing to take part, and are likely to remember details! Most importantly, make sure you have talked to them in outline about what you are doing, and that they know what questions you will be asking them. If possible, get a copy of your questions to them in advance.

NOW... ABOUT YOUR WORLD WAR EXPERIENCES

Drawing up your questions

This is the hardest, and the most important, part of your work. First, write a list of the general subject areas you hope to learn about. Sort this into a sensible order. Then draw up your questions on each area. Make sure these are brief, clear and to the point. Avoid asking too many questions. Make each of them open-ended, giving your subjects a chance to really talk. If you ask questions that can be answered by one word, or by 'yes' or 'no', you won't learn much.

bulk of your work will be a 'write-up' of your interview(s), in which:
(a) you summarise, with quotes where relevant, what you have learnt
(b) you comment on what you have heard, comparing different views of the event or period that you have got from different people
(c) you compare the results of your findings with what you have researched from other sources, such as books and articles.

Conducting your interviews with a subject or group of subjects

Make sure you record your answers carefully. Use a cassette recorder if you can, as it will be hard to write down all of a reply, and notes can easily be confused. Make sure your subjects speak clearly, and ask them to repeat or explain more fully anything you don't understand.

Finishing off

Make sure you include all the important 'beginning and end' parts to your assignment:
— a title page
— a list of contents
— an introduction (in which you explain why you chose the topic and what you are trying to find out)
— a bibliography (in which you list your sources of information, including people)
— a conclusion (in which you explain whether you found out what you hoped to, and how your research could have been improved).

Writing up your research

If you simply produce a written version of your recorded interviews, this is called a transcript. This will be useful, and may well form an **appendix** to your assignment. The

12
South Africa in the 1980s

In this chapter, which takes the form of a single exercise, you are asked to compare a variety of different sources and apply the ideas you have studied earlier in this book.

Source 12a
(Illingworth, in the *Daily Mail* in 1964, comments on the South African government's imprisonment of Nelson Mandela. This is further explained in Source 12b).

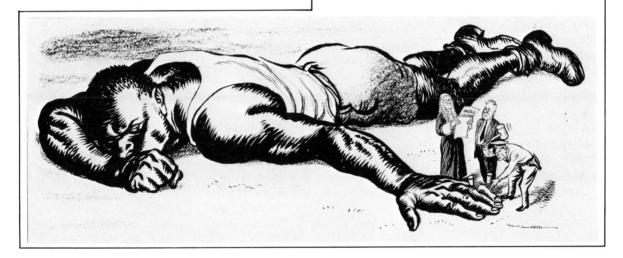

Source 12b
(*Encyclopaedia Britannica Yearbook*, 1964)

There was world-wide interest in the trial of eight members of the 'National Committee of Liberation' and the 'Spear of the Nation' who were arrested in 1963 at Johannesburg. Seven, including Nelson Mandela, were sentenced to life imprisonment; one was **acquitted**.

The government rejected pleas for **clemency** from the United Nations on the ground that the accused had received a fair trial by [the] court.

Acts of **sabotage** continued and a new underground organisation claimed responsibility. There were further banning orders, detentions and arrests. On 24 July a bomb explosion occurred in the central Johannesburg railway station, causing many injuries and resulting in one death.

Source 12c

(Dr C P Mulder, South African Minister of Information writing in *Progress through Separate Development*, published by the South African Department of Information in 1973)

'We believe that there are well-founded differences between people, which do not make them superior or inferior to one another, but distinctly different from one another. These differences, if not guided carefully with tact and wisdom, will cause friction and may even flare up in war and bloodshed. These differences may be in religion as in India and Pakistan, or in Northern Ireland; in language, as in Belgium, Switzerland or Canada; in color and race, as in the United States; in culture and custom, as found amongst the various tribes in a whole number of African countries like Nigeria, Somalia, Ethiopia, Kenya and others.

In South Africa we have a combination of all the differences mentioned above, i.e., religion, language, color, race, culture and customs. It must therefore follow that South Africa has more potential for strife and friction than most countries of the world. And yet very few countries can equal South Africa's record of peaceful coexistence, stability, economic growth and high standard of living for all its peoples, comparatively speaking.'

Nelson Mandela

President P. W. Botha

Source 12d

(*Daily Mail*, 1985)

President Botha has made some liberal reforms. He has even offered to release South Africa's top black nationalist political prisoner, Nelson Mandela, if he [gives up] violence.

But the situation, sadly, has gone far beyond that. The frustrated blacks now want nothing less than total power in South Africa . . .

Probably, step by step, the government will quell the unrest by sheer force, and peace, of a sort, will return to South Africa.

But it will be the sort of temporary calm that you get by screwing down the lid of a pressure cooker.

There will be no permanent solution to violence in South Africa until there is a political settlement between blacks and whites.

President Botha, while moving towards that goal, simply has not moved fast enough.

Source 12e

(*Sunday Telegraph*, July 1985)

Better **apartheid** than black revolution: that should be the Western message at the present time.

South Africa could be on the edge of a race war which would be disastrous for all races. At present, it seems that the West feels it can do nothing more constructive than try to pressurise Mr Botha into giving way. Down this path disaster lies. Apartheid in its present form is less evil than black revolution in its present form.

Anti-racism today threatens to become the new fanaticism which causes people to take leave of their senses in great matters as well as small.

(Findings of the Opinion Polls taken for *The Sunday Times*, 3 August 1986)

Blacks turn against violence

by Peter Godwin

MOST BLACKS in South Africa oppose violence, according to a poll carried out for The Sunday Times in the past month, despite their strong opposition to apartheid. Our poll found that nearly two thirds of blacks think violence is *not* justified to change apartheid, even though 88% are fairly or very unhappy with the racial system.

Even among blacks in urban areas, where most of the violence has taken place in the past 18 months, there is still a clear majority against violence, with 43% of blacks there saying that violence is justified and 55% saying it is not.

Despite the present level of violence, more blacks (50%) expect to see a peaceful solution to South Africa's problems rather than a plunge into civil war. But the urban blacks, who have witnessed most of the violence, take a much more pessimistic view than blacks who live in the countryside: some 63% of urban blacks think there will be a civil war.

The Sunday Times poll is the first country-wide survey of blacks in South Africa. Previous polls (including a survey carried out for this newspaper last August) have been limited to urban blacks because of the practical

Q: Do you think violence is justified to change the apartheid system?

	All blacks
Violence justified	28%
Violence not justified	63%
No opinion	9%

difficulties of polling in the countryside. Although our poll reveals that rural blacks are less militant than urban blacks, it also shows that they are far more ignorant of what is happening.

When asked to name the president of South Africa, 34% of rural blacks did not know the answer (compared with only 7% of urban blacks). In reply to our question "Have you heard of the phrase one-man-one-vote?", more than half the rural blacks polled had no idea what it meant.

Indeed, 41% of rural blacks have not heard of the state of emergency, 42% of them have not heard about possible economic sanctions against South Africa and 14% have never even heard of Nelson Mandela, the jailed African

National Congress leader. Urban blacks are far better informed on all these issues.

The poll gives little comfort to President P W Botha's hopes of encouraging blacks to join in limited power-sharing in government. Almost twice as many blacks are against working within the system as those who agree with it. Even the rural blacks, the government's main hope in setting up black councils, oppose such cooperation. This evidence is hardly likely to encourage the moderate Zulu leader, Chief Buthelezi, to take part in Botha's proposed National Statutory Council.

When asked if whites should have any special privileges in a new system of government in South Africa, only 1% of blacks believe they should. But most are happy for whites to stay on in any post-apartheid South Africa. Some 78% of blacks polled believe whites should continue to live in a future South Africa, whatever shape it takes.

By contrast, 53% of whites polled think that special white voting privileges are a good idea, with only 30% believing in equal voting rights for all races.

Black support for Mandela remains overwhelming despite his continued imprisonment. Over the past year, his support in urban areas has grown from 49% to 64%. Nationwide, Mandela has almost three times the support of the Zulu chief, Gatsha Buthelezi. Mandela is even the favourite for president among rural blacks. Buthelezi's popularity in urban areas is tiny by contrast.

The blacks' choices for leader

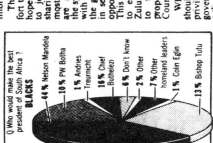

Q: Who would make the best president of South Africa?

BLACKS

- 44% Nelson Mandela
- 10% PW Botha
- 1% Andries Treurnicht
- 16% Chief Buthelezi
- 6% Don't know
- 2% Other
- 7% Other homeland leaders
- 1% Colin Eglin
- 13% Bishop Tutu

In the main cities he attracts only 5% of votes. South Africa's controversial state of emergency is strongly disliked by most blacks: 59% hate it. But in urban areas where it has most

Q: Do you think that South Africa's problems will be solved:

	Whites	Blacks
Peacefully	55%	50%
By civil war	32%	42%
No opinion	13%	8%

effect, that figure rises to 90%.

IN WHITE eyes, the president, P W Botha, is still the man they most want to lead them. Although his lead has fallen marginally since a year ago, at 62% he still has no serious challenger. The far right, represented by Eugene Terreblanche and Andries Treurnicht, attract only a total of 7% support.

Indeed, Buthelezi has almost twice as many white supporters as the white right-wing. After Botha himself, Buthelezi is apparently the great white hope. His white support has grown from 4% last year to 12% now.

On the crucial question of white willingness to accept eventual black rule in a democratic South Africa, the chasm remains as wide as ever with no evidence of the "leap of imagination" that Sir Geoffrey Howe, the foreign secretary, said last week was desperately needed from South African whites.

When given the choice between living under black rule or breaking away into a "white homeland" in some sort of federation, 50% choose the latter. Only 15%

Q: Do you think the British government supports or opposes apartheid?

	Whites	Blacks
Supports apartheid	7%	33%
Opposes apartheid	68%	24%
Don't know	25%	43%

are prepared to consider life under a black president.

But when asked what they thought *would* happen, the percentage of whites who believe in a white homeland drops to 34% and those believing that they will end up under black rule rises to 30%. The poll also found that 72% of whites, a rise of 9% since last year, now believe that the apartheid system will not exist in a decade.

The number of whites intending to emigrate from South Africa remains constant, with 12% either very or fairly likely to leave within 10 years, a similar figure to that in last year's poll of whites. Obviously, some of those polled last year who may now have done so. But 76% of whites polled, including nearly all Afrikaners, show no intention of leaving.

How the poll was conducted

THE POLL was carried out for The Sunday Times by Market & Opinion Research International (Mori) and the South African company, Markinor, last month. The most difficult part of the operation was interviewing blacks in remote rural areas.

Interviewers, who were black, had to travel to a sampling point drawn up on a map, then walk to the nearest village or cluster of huts. Because of these difficulties, the polling results were seized by the police.

A representative sample of 615 blacks was interviewed between July 18-27 at 123 points throughout the country, covering urban areas and homelands, with the exception of the Transkei, where polling results were seized by the police.

Questionnaires were translated into local languages. Data was weighted to reflect the latest population estimates by age and language. Two hundred black were interviewed in the main metropolitan areas of Johannesburg, the Reef and Pretoria. They are directly comparable with the sample of 400 blacks interviewed for our poll in August 1985.

A representative sample of 500 whites was interviewed by telephone on July 26 and 27 in 100 sampling points.

61

Violence in the black townships has continued throughout the 1980s.

Exercises
1 Which of these sources would you regard as primary sources? Explain how you decided.
2 Which of these sources present you with:
   (a) fact(s) only
   (b) opinion(s) only
   (c) a mixture of fact and opinion
   Where necessary, explain your decisions.
3 Which of Sources 12a and 12b gives you a better understanding of Nelson Mandela's imprisonment in 1964? Explain your answer.

4 Compare Sources 12d and 12f. Do the findings of the opinion polls confirm or contradict the view of the *Daily Mail*?
5 Would Dr Mulder, the author of Source 12c, be more likely to agree with Source 12d or Source 12e? Explain how you decided.
6 If you had to decide which of these sources is the *most* reliable, and which the *least* reliable, which two sources would you choose, and why?
7 Find out in outline what the situation is in South Africa today. Have the views of any of the sources above come true?

Glossary

abdication — the act of giving up the throne

acquitted — found not guilty

aggression — attack

agrarian — agricultural

Anschluss — union

apartheid — system of keeping different races apart

appendix — addition at the end of a book

arrogant — big-headed; proud

artefact — something made by a human being

banshee — spirit whose wailing means there will soon be a death in the family

biased — one-sided

capitalist — rich business person

caprice — sudden change of mind without reason

censored — changed by having parts cut out

clemency — mercy

co-existence — existing together

commentary — words which accompany a film

communique — an official announcement

communism — system in which most property is owned by the state

contradict — disagree with; deny

covenant — solemn agreement

cultural — concerning the customs and arts of a race or nation

curfew — a time when people must stay indoors

decade — ten years

democracy — a government for which everyone may vote

descendant — offspring, such as child or grandchild

dictator — person who has total power over a country

diplomatic — to do with negotiations between countries

documentary — film showing real events

editorial — article in a newspaper, giving the newspaper's opinions

emblematical — symbolic

endorse — approve; support

entanglement — something hard to get through

entreat — beg

fundamental — basic

garb — clothing

heritage — what is handed on from past generations

intriguing — plotting

invoke — appeal for

kulak — rich peasant

latrine — toilet

legion — army

liberation — setting free

manifesto — a statement of what a political party will do if it is elected

media — the means of communication (e.g. TV, radio)

memoirs — a person's account of his or her own life

minutes — record of what happened at a meeting

misinformation — lies

morale — people's courage, confidence and enthusiasm

mutiny	rebellion by soldiers or sailors
narrative	story
neutral	not biased
optimistic	hoping for the best
pact	agreement
pessimistic	expecting the worst
prejudice	opinion without good reason
prominent	well-known
propaganda	methods of spreading opinions, and getting people to believe them
propagandist	person who produces propaganda
regime	system of government
Reich	German empire
resignation	act of giving up a job
sabotage	destruction
sadism	love of cruelty
statesmen	people skilled in running public affairs
statistics	facts expressed in numbers
staunchest	the most strong
stormtroopers	brown-shirted Nazi troops
Suffragette	supporter of votes for women
technological	to do with using science for business or industry
torpedoed	hit by an explosive submarine weapon
traitor	person who betrays his/her country
venerates	worships

Index